TEXTBOOK OF EXTENSION EDUCATION

SATWIK SAHAY BISARYA

Contents

Preface

This book is intended for the college students who may not yet encountered a course in extension education. Thus, it is really an "Introduction" to extension education. It is not intended to develop any new theories but introduce the students with the existing knowhow in this area. Extension Education courses have been introduced in most of the agricultural universities for students of agriculture, horticulture , forestry, home science, veterinary science, dairy science, engineering and fisheries. The Indian council of Agricultural Research has recently revised the syllabus for the graduate students and added new dimensions to the courses. This syllabus is made common for all the universities in India. With the inclusion of new courses in the syllabus the old books on this subject became obsolete. The need for new books with recent concepts and information became the need of the hour. It is hoped that this book will be helpful to these students in a preliminary understanding of this subject.

Large number of rural development programmes are being undertaken by the government, corporate and private sectors for the upliftment of the masses. However, there is always dearth of good extension workers and entrepreneurs to manage these programmes. This book is expected to provide guideline to all those engaged in the task of rural upliftment. This book will help in understanding the concepts, philosophy, objectives and methods of working with the rural people.

In the preparation of this book, benefit of the valuable work of outstanding scholars and other publications was taken. Without their original efforts, this text book could not have been written. I acknowledge with thanks this valuable debt and welcome any suggestions for the improvement of this book.

CHAPTER ONE

EDUCATION: MEANING, DEFINITION & TYPES

Education word is derived from the Latin root 'ex' meaning out and 'tension' meaning stretching. Education is the process of facilitating learning or acquisition of knowledge, skill values and habits. Under education method we can includes teaching training discussion, directed toward research. Education take place them self as well as in front of instructor Education can take place in formal or informal settings and any experience that has a formative effect on the way one thinks, feels, or acts may be considered education.

Definition of Education

- Education is the process of developing capability of the individual so that they can adequately response to their situation. We can also define education as process of bringing desirable change into the behaviour of human being.
- Webster defined education as the process of teaching to develop the knowledge, skill, or character of the student.

- "Sociologist Rodney Stark declares that, Education is the cheapest, most rapid and most reliable path to economic advancement under present conditions,"

Types of Education

There are mainly three types of education, namely, Formal, Informal and Non-formal. Each of these types is briefly described below.

(A) Formal Education

Formal education corresponds to a systematic, organized education model, structured and administered according to a given set of laws and norms, presenting a rather rigid curriculum as regards objectives, content and methodology. It is characterized by a contiguous education process named, as Sarramona remarks, "presential education", which necessarily involves the teacher, the students and the institution. It corresponds to the education process normally adopted by our schools and universities.

- Planned with a particular end in view.
- Limited to a specific period.
- Well-defined and systematic curriculum.
- Given by specially qualified teachers.
- Includes activities outside the classroom
- Observes strict discipline.

(B) Informal Education

Informal education is quite diverse from formal education and, particularly, from non- formal education, although in certain cases it is capable of maintaining a close relationship with both. It does not correspond to an organized and systematic view of education; informal education life long process in which portions azure's knowledge, skill, attitude and insight from daily experiences and exposure to the endearment at home.

- Incidental and spontaneous

- Not-pre-planned.

- Not imparted by any specialized agency.

- No prescribed time-table or curriculum.

- May be negative also

(C) Non-Formal Education

It is organized and systematic education activity carried on outside the frame work of the formal system to provide selected type of learning to the particular group of population.

- Derived from the expression 'formal education.

- Outside the realm of formal education.

- Conscious and deliberate.

- To be organized for a homogeneous group.

- Serving the need of the identified group.

References

1. Claudio Zaki Dib (1988). Formal, Non-Formal and Informal Education: Concepts/Applicability. Cooperative Networks in Physics Education - Conference Proceedings 173", American Institute of Physics, New York, pp. 300-315 retrieved from http://techne- dib.com.br/downloads/6.pdf

2. Dimensions Of Agricultural Extension:(Aext191) (1+1). Principles, Philosophy Processes And Objectives Of Extension Retrieved fromhttp://eagri.org/eagri50/AEXT191/lec02.pdf

3. Dushi Guari. Notes on the Types of education: formal, informal, non-formal. Retrieved from http://www.preservearticles.com/

notes/notes-on-the-types-of-education-formal-informal-non-formal/17995

4. Education from Wikipedia retrieved from https://en.wikipedia.org/wiki/Education

5. Fundamental of Rural Sociology & Educational Psychology, (AEXT391) (2+0), lect1 retrieved fromhttp://eagri.org/eagri50/AEXT391/lec01.pdf

6. Principles of Extension Education, Dairy Extension Education. Retrieved from http://ecoursesonline.iasri.res.in/mod/resource/view.php?id=4360

7. Ray. G.L.(2013) Extension Communication and management. New Delhi. Kalayni publication.

8. Sharma, A. (Sep 8, 2016). Education: Meaning, Definition, types of education and characteristics, Extension education: Meaning, definition and concept. Retrieved from https://www.slideshare.net/Arpita615/education-meaning-definition-types-of-education-and- characteristicsextension-education-meaning-definition-and-concept

CHAPTER TWO

EXTENSION EDUCATION

The use of the term 'extension' originated in England in 1866 with a system of university extension which was taken up first by Cambridge and Oxford Universities, and later by other educational institutions in England and in other countries. The term 'extension education' was first used in 1873 by Cambridge University to take the educational advantages of universities to ordinary people. There are many experts and practitioners who have defined and opined extension in various ways encompassing many facets of extension's functions. Extension means that type of education which is stretched out to the people in rural areas, beyond the limits of the educational institutions to which the formal type of education is normally confined.

Basic Definitions Related to Extension

- Extension education is an applied social science consisting of relevant content derived from physical, biological and social sciences and in its own process synthesized into a body of knowledge, concepts, principles and procedures oriented to provide non-credit out of school education largely for adults. - *Leagans (1971)*
- Extension Education is a science, which deals with the creation, transmission & application of knowledge designed to bring

about planned changes in the behavior-complex of people, with a view to help them live better by learning the ways of improving their vocations, enterprises & institutions. *(Reddy, 1993)*

- Extension Education is a science that brings about desirable changes in the behavior of the concerned persons through educational methods, so as to improve their general standard of living with their own efforts. In fact, it deals with the designs & strategies of transfer of technology to the concerned persons. In other words, what is taught to the farmers is not Extension Education, though its knowledge is applied for the effective & efficient communication of various programmes of change. *(Singh, 1994)*

- Extension is education and that its purpose is to change attitude and practices of the people with whom the work is to change. *(Ensminger,1957)*

- Extension Education is the process of teaching rural people how to live better by learning ways to improve their farm, home and community institutions. *(Leagans, 1961)*

- Extension an out of school education and services for the members of the farm family and others directly or indirectly engaged in farm production to enable them to adopt improved practices in production, management, conservation and marketing. Several authors defined extension in various ways emphasizing the importance of one or the other aspect of extension. *(National Commission on Agriculture, 1976)*

Scope of Extension Education

Extension appears to have unlimited scope in situations where there is need for creating awareness amongst the people and changing their behavior by informing and educating them. Kelsey and Hearne (1967) identified nine areas of programme emphasis, which indicate the scope of agricultural extension.

1. Efficiency in agricultural production.
2. Efficiency in marketing, distribution and utilization.

3. Conservation, development and use of natural resources.
4. Management on the farm and in the home.
5. Family living.
6. Youth development.
7. Leadership development.
8. Community development and rural area development.
9. Public affairs.

The following statements will further amplify the scope of extension.

1. Extension is fundamentally a system of out-of-school education for adults and youths alike. It is a system where people are motivated through a proper approach to help themselves by applying science in their daily lives, in farming, home making and community living.
2. Extension is education for all village people.
3. Extension is bringing about desirable changes in the knowledge, attitudes and skills of people.
4. Extension is helping people to help themselves.
5. Extension is working with men and women, boys and girls, to answer their felt needs and wants.
6. Extension is teaching through "learning by doing" and "seeing is believing".
7. Extension is working in harmony with the culture of the people.
8. Extension is a two-way channel; it brings scientific information to village people and it also takes the Problems of the village people to the scientific institutes for solution.
9. Extension is working together (in groups) to expand the welfare and happiness of the people with their own families, their own villages, their own country and the world.
10. Extension is development of individuals in their day-to-day living, development of their leaders, their society and their world as a whole.

Principal of Extension Education

Principles are generalized guidelines, which form the basis for decision and action in a consistent way. The universal truth in extension, which have been observed and found to hold good under varying conditions and circumstances are presented.

Principle of peoples need and interest

Extension work must be based on the needs & interests of the people. Always programme must be develop according needs & interests these need differ from individual to individual, from village to village, from block to block, from state to state; therefore, there cannot be one programme for all people.

Principle of grass root level organisation

A group of rural people in local community should sponsor extension work. They work with local community so that the programme should fit in with the local conditions. The aim of organising the local group is to demonstrate the value of the new practices or programmes so that more & more people would participate.

Principle of cultural difference

Extension work is based on the cultural background of the people with whom the work is done. Differences in the culture are always being there between extension worker and rural people, success is when extension professionals has to know the level of the knowledge, & the skills of the people, methods & tools used by them, their customs, traditions, beliefs, values, etc. before starting the extension programme.

Principle of cooperation and peoples participation

Extension is a co-operative venture. It is a joint democratic enterprise in which rural people co- operate with their village, block & state officials to pursue a common cause. Ultimately without the cooperation of people the work cannot be successful and desired result cannot be achieved. The first task of extension education is the cooperation of people and their participation in work. Extension helps people to help themselves. Good extension work is directed towards assisting rural families to work out their own problems rather than giving them ready-made solutions. Actual participation & experience of people in these programmes creates self-confidence in them and also they learn more by doing. People should realise that the task of extension education is their own task. Participation in extension work generates confidence among people for the work. It is not essential that all the members of the society should participate but Extension professionals should try for maximum participation of people.

Principle of cultural change

Extension education starts with what the learner knows, has and thinks. With this in mind and with an attitude of respect towards clients, the extension professionals must seek to discover and understand the limitations, taboo and the cultural values related to each phase of programme so that an acceptable approach could be selected in the locality.

Principle of learning by doing

According to this principle, farmers are encouraged to learn by doing the work themselves and by participating in it. When a person does a work, he gains practical knowledge and experiences the difficulties. Extension professionals are able to understand the problems and provide proper guidance to the farmers and thus, they are able to receive proper information/feedback.

Principle of trained specialists

It is very difficult that extension personnel should be knowledgeable about all problems. Therefore, it is necessary that specialists should impart training to the farmers from time to time.

Principle of adaptability in use of extension teaching methods

People differ from each other, one group differs from another group and conditions also differ from place to place. An extension programme should be flexible, so that necessary changes can be made whenever needed, to meet the varying conditions. Extension professionals should have knowledge of extension methods so that they can select proper method according to the condition. Teaching methods should be flexible so that they can be properly applied on people according to their age groups, educational background, economic standard and gender. In extension education, two or more methods should be applied according to the principle of adaptability.

Principle of leadership

Extension work is based on the full utilisation of local leadership. The selection & training of local leaders to enable them to help in carrying out extension work is essential to the success of the programme. People have more faith in local leaders & they should be used to put across a new idea so that it is accepted with the least resistance.

Principle of whole family

Extension work will have a better chance of success if the extension professionals have a whole-family approach instead of piecemeal approach or separate & uninterested approach. Extension work is, therefore, for the whole family, i.e. for male, female and children.

Principle of evaluation

Extension is based upon the methods of science, and it needs constant evaluation. The effectiveness of the work is measured in terms of the changes brought about in the knowledge, skill, attitude, and adoption behaviour of the people, not merely in terms of achievement of physical targets.

Principle of satisfaction

The end-product of the effort of extension teaching is the satisfaction that comes to the farmer and his family members as the result of solving a problem, meeting a need, acquiring a new skill or some other changes in behaviour. Satisfaction is the key to success in extension work. A satisfied stakeholder is the best advertisement.

Principal of Indigenous Knowledge

People everywhere have indigenous knowledge system which they have develop through generation of work experience and problem solving in their own specific situation. The indigenous knowledge systems encompass all aspect of life and people considered it essential for their survival.

Objective of Extension

Objectives are expression of the ends towards which our efforts are directed.

Fundamental objective: The fundamental objective of extension is the development of the people or the "Destination man". In other words, it is to develop the rural people economically, socially and culturally by means of education. Eg.: To increase socio- economic status and standard of living of Indian farming Community.

General objectives (Function): The general objectives of the extension are

- To assist people to discover and analyze their problems, their felt and unfelt needs.
- To develop leadership among people and help them in organizing groups to solve their problems.
- To disseminate information based on research and /or practical experience, in such a manner that the people would accept it and put it into actual practice.
- To keep the research workers informed of the peoples' problems from time to time, so that they may offer solutions based on necessary research.

- To assist people in mobilising and utilizing the resources which they have and which they need from outside. Eg.: To increase the a production and productivity of Paddy in India.

Working objectives: Is one which focuses on specific activity of a specific group in a selected geographic area. Eg.: To increase the yield of PKM-1 of the tomato among the tomato growers of Madhukkarai block in Coimbatore District.

The major objectives of Extension may also be categorized as follows:

1. Material - increase production, income.

2. Educational - change the outlook of people or develop the individuals.
3. Social and cultural - development of the community.

Extension Educational Process

An effective extension educational programme involves five essential and interrelated steps. This concept of the extension educational process is intended only to clarify the steps necessary in carrying out a planned educational effort. It does not imply that these steps are definitely separate from each other. Experience shows that planning, teaching and evaluation take place continuously, in varying degrees, throughout all phases of extension activities

First step: The first step consists of collection of facts and analysis of the situation. Facts about the people and their enterprises; the economic, social, cultural, physical and technological environment in which they live and work. These may be obtained by appropriate survey and establishing rapport with the people.

The responses obtained are to be analyzed with the local people to identify the problems and resources available in the community. For example, after a survey in a community and analysis of the data, the problem was identified as low income of the farm family from their crop production enterprise.

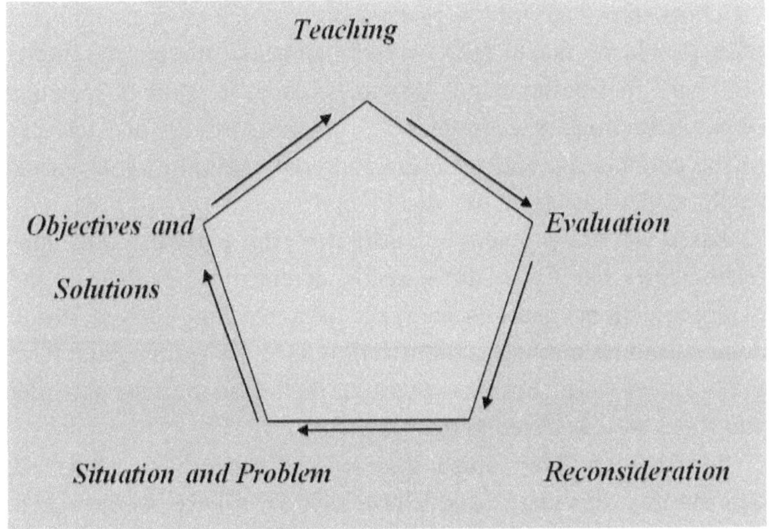

Extension Educational Process

Second step: The next step is deciding on realistic objectives which may be accomplished by the community. A limited number of objectives should be selected by involving the local people. The objectives should be specific and clearly stated, and on completion should bring satisfaction to the community. Objectives should state the behavioral changes in people as well as economic and social outcomes desired.

In the example, the problem was identified as low income from the crop production enterprise. A deeper probe into the date revealed that low income was due to low yield of crops, which was

attributed to the use of local seeds with low yield potential, application of little fertilizer and lack of protection measures. By taking into consideration the capacity and competency of the people in the community and the availability of resources, the objective was 1 3 4 5 2 set up to increase the crop yield by 20 per cent within a certain period of time. It was estimated that the increased yield shall bring increased income, which shall enhance the family welfare.

Third step: The third step is teaching, which involves choosing what should be taught (the content) and how the people should be taught the methods and aids to be used. It requires selecting research findings of economic and practical importance relevant to the community, and selection and combination of appropriate teaching methods and aids.

Based on the problems identified in the particular example, technologies like use of HYV seeds, application of fertilizer and plant protection chemicals were selected as teaching content. Result demonstration, method demonstration, farmers' training and farm publications were chosen as teaching methods, and tape recorder and slides were selected as teaching aids.

Fourth step: The fourth step is evaluating the teaching i.e, determining the extent to which the objectives have been reached. To evaluate the results of an educational programme objectively, it is desirable to conduct a re-survey. The evidence of changed behavior should be collected, which shall not only provide a measure of success, but shall also indicate the deficiencies, if any.

In the example, the re-survey after the fixed period of time, indicated that the crop yield had increased by 10 percent. It, therefore, indicated that there was a gap of 10 per cent in crop yield in comparison to the target (objective) of 20 per cent fixed earlier. The re-survey also indicated that there had been two important deficiencies in carrying out the extension educational program, such as, there was lack of proper water management and the farmers could not apply the fertilizer and plant protection chemicals as per recommendation due to lack of funds.

Fifth step: The fifth step is re-consideration of the entire extension educational programme on the light of the results of evaluation. The problems identified in the process of evaluation may become the starting point for the next phase of the extension educational programme, unless new problems have developed or new situations have arisen.

After re-consideration of the results of evaluation with the people, the following teaching objectives were again set up. For example, they were, training the farmers on proper water practices and putting up demonstrations on water management. The people were also advised to contact the banks for obtaining production credit in time to purchase critical inputs. Thus, the continuous process of extension education shall go on, resulting in progress of the people from a less desirable to a more desirable situation.

References

1. Claudio Zaki Dib (1988). Formal, Non-Formal and Informal Education: Concepts/Applicability. Cooperative Networks in Physics Education - Conference Proceedings 173", American Institute of Physics, New York, pp. 300-315 retrieved from http://techne- dib.com.br/downloads/6.pdf
2. Dimensions Of Agricultural Extension:(Aext191) (1+1). Principles, Philosophy Processes And Objectives Of Extension Retrieved fromhttp://eagri.org/eagri50/AEXT191/lec02.pdf
3. Dushi Guari. Notes on the Types of education: formal, informal, non-formal. Retrieved from http://www.preservearticles.com/notes/notes-on-the-types-of-education-formal-informal-non-formal/17995
4. Education from Wikipedia retrieved from https://en.wikipedia.org/wiki/Education
5. Fundamental of Rural Sociology & Educational Psychology, (AEXT391) (2+0), lect1 retrieved fromhttp://eagri.org/eagri50/AEXT391/lec01.pdf
6. Principles of Extension Education, Dairy Extension Education. Retrieved from http://ecoursesonline.iasri.res.in/mod/resource/view.php?id=4360
7. Ray. G.L.(2013) Extension Communication and management. New Delhi. Kalayni publication.

CHAPTER THREE

EXTENSION PROGRAMME PLANNING

The first step in any systematic attempt to promote rural development is to prepare useful programmes based on people needs. The development of such programmes, require planning which harmonize with the local needs as the people see them and with the national interests with which the country as a whole is concerned, is an important responsibility of extension personnel at all levels- national, state, district, block & village.

Programme planning is the process of making decisions about the direction & intensity of extension-education efforts of extension-service to bring about social, economic & technological changes.

Program planning is a process which involves multiple steps including the identification of a problem, selection of desired outcomes, assessment of available resources, implementation and evaluation of the program. In other words it is a procedure of working with the people to recognize unsatisfactory situations or problems and to determine possible solutions.

According to Kelsey and Hearne (1967) An Extension Porgramme is a statement of situation, objective, problems and solutions. It is relatively permanent but requires constant revision.

Leagans (1961) says that an "extension programme" is a set of clearly defined, consciously conceived objectives or ends, derived from an adequate analysis of the situation, which are to be achieved through extension teaching activity'.

Lawrence (1962) says that an "extension programme" is the sum total of all the activities and undertakings of a county extension services. It includes: (i) programme planning process (ii) written programme statement (iii) plan of work (iv) programme execution (v) results and (vi) evaluation.

Programme planning: Programme planning is a decision making process which involves critical analysis of the existing problems and evaluation of available best alternatives to solve these problems by cooperative efforts of the people for community growth and development.

Some relevant terms required to understand in programme planning given below:

Programme: Programme is a written statement which describes proposed developmental activities, the problems they address, the actions, and resources required.

Planning: it is a process which involves studying the past and present in order to forecast the future and in the light of that forecast determining he goal to be achieved.

Plan: Plan is schedule of development work outlining different activities in a specific period. It answers the questions like what, why, how, and when as well as by whom and where the work is to be done.

Aims: Aims are generalized and broad statement of directions with respect to given activities. eg. The improvement of farmers' economic condition.

Objectives: Objectives are expression of ends towards which our efforts are directed. The dictionary meaning of objective is 'something that one's efforts or actions are intended to attain or accomplish'

e.g. To increase the yield of rice by 30 percent.

Goal: Goal is the distance in any given direction one expects to go during a given period of time e.g. to increase yield of rice by 10 quintals per hectare in the current year.

Problem: It refers to a situation, condition, or issue that is yet unresolved and after study people decided need to change it.

Solution: Solution is a course of proposed action to change an unsatisfactory condition to one that is more satisfying.

Project: it is a specification of work to be done or procedures to be followed in order to accomplish a particular objective.

Plan: It is a predetermined course of action.

Plan of work: it is an outline of activities so arranged as to enable efficient execution of the programme. The plan of work indicates what, who, how and when the activities will carried out.

Calendar of Work: Calendar of work is a plan of activities to be undertaken in a particular time sequence.

Objectives of Programme

The general objective of an extension programme is to influence people to transform their life in better way. The assumption is that there is a need for change and make people aware are of this, if they are not and to develop their needs. Important objectives of having a programme planning as per Kelsey and Hearne (1966) are as follows:

1. To ensure careful consideration of what is to be done and why.
2. To furnish a guide against which to judge all new proposals.
3. To establish objectives toward which progress can be measured and evaluated.
4. To have a means of choosing the important (deep rooted) from incidental (less important) problems; and the permanent from the temporary changes.
5. To develop a common understanding about the means and ends between functionaries and organizations.
6. To ensure continuity during changes of personnel.

7. To help develop leadership.

8. To avoid wastage of time & money and promote efficiency.

9. To justify expenditure and to ensure flow of funds.

10. To have a statement in written form for public use.

Principles of Extension Programme Planning

Extension programmes have the definite purpose of improving rural life through individual, group and community action. Extension programme planning has certain principles, which holds good irrespective of the nature of the clientele, and the enterprises they may be pursuing, viz.:

1. Extension programmes should be based on an analysis of the past experiences, present situation and future needs. For programme determination adequate information about the people and their situation have to be collected. The present information is to be analyses and interpreted on the basis of past experiences, by taking local people into confidence. This shall help in arriving at the future needs

2. Extension programmes should have clear and significant objectives, which could satisfy important needs of the people. The main objective of programme development is to satisfy the need of people. For this purpose significant objectives pertaining to important needs of the people should be selected and clearly stated. The emphasis will be on what is attainable rather than on what is ideal although one should not lose sight of the ideal.

3. Extension programmes should fix up priority on the basis of available resources and time. Generally in developed countries rural people have multiple problems but at the same time all problems cannot be taken up for solution because of limitation of the available resources. Therefore considering this fact

priority should be decided in the programme.

4. Extension programmes should clearly indicate the availability and utilization of resources. To make programme practical and workable it is important to clearly indicate the availability of funds, facilities, supplies and the needed personnel and how these resources will be utilized.

5. Extension programmes should have a general agreement at various levels. Programme prepared at various levels such as village, district, state and national levels. The extension programme of any department or level should not be conflict or contradict with the extension programme of the any other department or level.

6. Extension programmes should involve people at the local level. Extension programme are implemented at local level. Therefore, local people should be involved in all stages starting from programme formulation to programme implementation.

7. Extension programmes should involve relevant institutions and organization. Extension programme cannot be implemented in isolation. It requires the support of many institution and organizations. The programme should broadly indicate the institutions and organizations to be involved and how they shall contribute in attaining the programme objectives.

8. Extension programme should have definite plan of work. The plan of work may be separately drawn up or incorporated in the programme. The programme should at least broadly indicate how it will be executed.

9. Extension programme should provide for evaluation of results and reconsideration of the programme. The programme should make provision for periodical monitoring and evaluation of results to judge its progress. On the basis of the findings of evaluation the programme should be suitably modified for attainment of objectives within the stipulated time.

10. Extension programmes should provide for equitable distribution of benefits amongst the members of the community. In community generally resource full persons benefited more

compared to resource poor in any programme. As this creates social disparity and social tension the planning of extension programmes should give adequate emphasis on the weaker section of the community.

Steps in Extension Programme Planning Process

The process of extension, as applied to development programmes, involves five essential phases (SOTER) i.e. Analyzing the Situation, Objectives or Goals to be Accomplished, Teaching, Evaluating the Teaching, Reconsidering (Leagans, 1961). These steps are intended only to clarify the necessary actions in carrying out a planned extension educational effort.

The program development process is on-going and continuous. Each educational initiative, workshop or event we carry out modifies the initial situation. As a consequence, any plan of action continues to evolve and change as the situation or context changes.

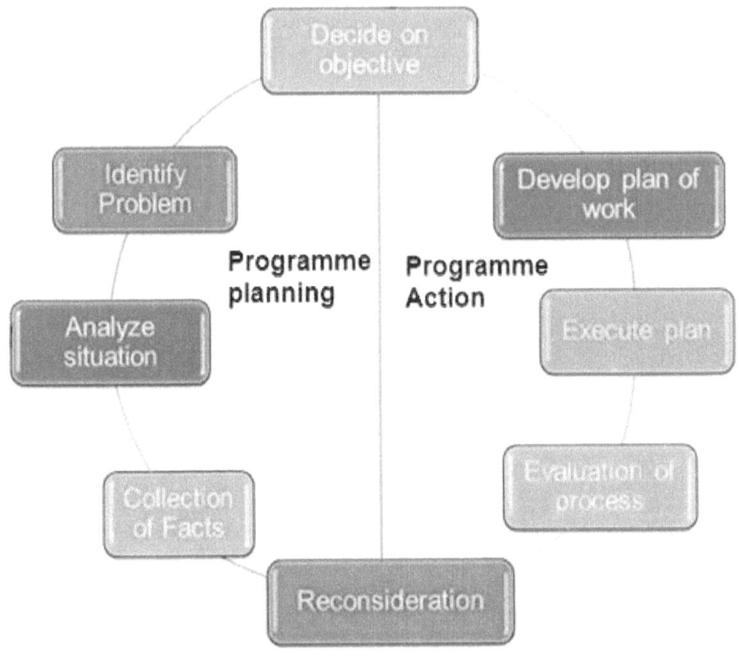

Steps of Programme Planning

Collection of facts

Sound plans are based on availability of relevant & reliable facts. This includes facts about the village people, physical conditions, existing farm & home practices, trends & outlook. Besides, other facts about customs, traditions, rural institutions, peoples' organisations operating in the area, etc. should be collected. The tools & techniques for collecting data include systematic observations, a questionnaire, interviews & surveys, existing governmental records, census reports, reports of the Planning Commission, Central Bureau of Statistics, and the past experiences of people.

Analysis of the situation

After collecting facts, they are analysed and interpreted to find out the problems & needs of the people.

Identification of problems

As a result of the analysis of facts, the important gaps between 'what is' & 'what ought to be' are identified and the problems leading to such a situation are located. These gaps represent the people's needs.

Determination of objectives

Once the needs & problems of the people have been identified, they are stated in terms of objectives & goals. The objectives represent a forecast of the changes in the behaviour of the people and the situation to be brought about. The objectives may be long-term as well as short-term, and must be stated clearly.

Developing the plan of work

In order to achieve the stated objectives & goals, the means & methods attaining each objective are selected; and the action plan, i.e. the calendar of activities is developed. It includes the technical content, who should do what, and the time-limit within the work will be completed. The plan of work may be seasonal, short-term, annual or long-term.

Execution of the plan of work

Once the action plan has been developed, arrangement for supplying the necessary inputs, credits, teaching aids, extension literature etc. has to be made and the specific action has to be initiated. The execution of the plan of work is to be done through extension methods for stimulating individuals and groups to think, act and participate effectively. People should be involved at every step to ensure the success of the programme.

Evaluation

It is done to measure the degree of success of the programme in terms of the objectives & goals set forth. This is basically done to determine the changes in the behaviour of the people as a result of the extension programme. The evaluation is done not only of the physical achievements but also of the methods & techniques used and of the other steps in the programme planning process, so that the strong & weak points may be identified and necessary changes may be incorporated accordingly.

Reconsideration

The systematic and periodic evaluation of the programme will reveal the weak and strong points of the programme. Based on these points, the programme is reconsidered and the necessary adjustments & changes are made in order to make it more meaningful & sound.

Programme planning is not the end-product of extension activities, but it is an educational tool for helping people to identify their own problems and make timely & judicious decisions. From the above mentioned cycle, it is clear that the planning of an extension programme comprises a logical series of consecutive steps. The first 4 steps form the programme-phase. The steps 5-7 form the action- phase. The step 8, i.e. reconsideration, joins the 2 phases together, where it leads to the fact- collecting step, thus beginning once more the never ending or continuous process of planning the extension programme.

References:

1. Ahmed, M. R. (1991. Planning and Designing Social Forestry Project. In Ahmed, M. R. (ed.) Social Forestry and Community Development, pp. 109 - 116. FAO, FTPP.
2. Extension Program Planning and Evaluation. (2020 Jan. 10). retrieved from http://eagri.org/eagri50/AEXT392/lec02.html
3. Legans J.P. (1961). Characteristics of Teaching and Learning in Extension Education, Extension Teaching Methods, The Communication Process and Programme Planning to Meet People's Needs in Extension Education in Community Development . Directorate of Extension, Govt. of India, New Delhi.
4. Programme planning. (2020 Jan. 15) retrieved from http://ecoursesonline.iasri.res.in/mod/resource/view.php?id=4384
5. Ray G. L. (2017). Extension Communication and Management. New Delhi, Kalyani Publisher. Pp 227-248
6. Sandhu A. S. (2003). Extension Programme Planning. New Delhi, Oxford and IBH Publishers.
7. Sasidhar P V (2019Dec .21 .)Programme Planning .retrieved http//:www.egyankosh.ac.in/bitstream/123456789/39227/1/Unit-1.pdf
8. Van den Ban, A.W. and Hawkins, H.S. (2002). Agricultural Extension, New Delhi, CBS Publishers and Distributors.

CHAPTER FOUR

EXTENSION SYSTEM IN INDIA

Rural development is an obligation of the Government to raise the standard of living of the rural people. World Bank defined rural development in terms of an improvement of the economic and social life of the rural poor. Rural development encompasses all sectors of rural life. In its widest sense, it implies development of every aspect of rural life. There are number of rural development programs were started by the Nationalists and Social reformers. Some of these programs gradually disappeared or some were merged with Government sponsored schemes later. 'This is because of various reasons like lack of encouragement of the Government, lack of financial support, inadequate, in experienced and untrained staff. For the clarity, we can divide these Development Programmes in two parts: Pre-Independence Programmes, and Post-Independence Programmes.

Pre-independence era Programmes:-

1. Sriniketan Project

In 1920, Rabindra Nath Tagore laid the foundation of theSriniketan Institute for Rural Reconstruction with the help of sociologist Shri L.M. Hurst. and formulated aprogramme for the all- round improvement in the Village of hisZamindari with the objective of studying rural problems and ofhelping the

Villagers to develop agriculture, improving thelivestock, formation of co- operatives. He believed in self help and mutual help and wanted the village workers to be involved in the life of rural people and work for their welfare. He started this programme in the cluster of **8 Villages** but were not very successful and can only be described as rural welfare works.

The absence of market facilities, professional guidance, lack of co-ordination between the implementing authority and improper incentives for workers made the task more difficult and desired results could not be achieved

1. Gurgaon experiment

In 1920, Mr. Brayne had been appointed on the post of Deputy Commissioner in Gurgaon district and he began this project of rural upliftment in his district, which became famous as "Gurgaon Project." The programme aimed at improving agriculture, education, health and sanitation facilities, co-operation, and social development with greater vigor. He stressed on the dignity of labour, selfhelp and conducted propaganda through films, songs, skits and plays with a view to increase farm yields and improving health standards. Although this project got some success yet this scheme also could not survive more because this project was also based upon the sentiments of F.L. Brayne and when he was transferred, gradually this programme also stopped.

2. Marthandam Project

Dr. Spencer Hatch of the **Young Men's Christian Association (YMCA)** set up a Project in 1921 at Martandam, 25 miles south of Thiruvananthapuram. The purpose of this experiment was to bring about a complete upward development towards a more complete and meaningful life for rural people three folded development **-spirit, mind and body.** To achieve this they launched five sided programme-spiritual, mental, physical, economic and social development were also included. The main stress in programme was on the principle that people should not

depend on Government for support because when concessions and help in any field are not given, the people develop in them a feeling of self-help and self- reliance.

The objectives of this programme was the YMCA should work in the Villages to eliminate poverty. For the Rural Demonstration Centre at Martandam had a demonstration farm, prized animals, equipment for the honey industry and other cottage vocations.

3. Firka Development scheme

The Firka Development scheme of Madras was a Government sponsored Scheme in 1946 this programme aimed at organizing the villagers for a happier, more prosperous and fuller life in which the individual villagers had the opportunity to develop both as an individual and as a unit of a well- integrated society. Among Pre-Independence project, this was the biggest project. Selection of Firkas- based on general backwardness of the area and where there is possibility of initiating cottage industries. The priority areas of work for each Firka included Rural reconstruction facility, Drinking water facility, Sanitation Khadi and other village industries.

For the overall development of the area planning was framed in two categories

- Short term plans (development of infrastructure, communications)

- Long term plans (knowledge inputs, attainment of Gandhian ideal)

Post- Independence Era Programme

Etawah Pilot Project :- In 1947, after Independence, the Government of India prioritised on rural development and how this work should be managed. For this the guidance of an experienced person was needed. The Government of India urged the U.S. government to send Mr. Albert Mayor to India because he had enough experience of rural development programme and was a Rural Sociologist.

Under the leadership of **Lt.Col.Albert Mayor of USA** , the office of **Etawah Pilot Project** was established by the U.P Govt. in October 1948 at Mahewa in the Etawah District. Initially 64 villages were selected around Mahewa District for the development. It was also called **Average District Plan** because the project was initiated in the normal envoirnment . This programme named as pilot project means the work is for specific location and further it shows the path.This progrrame was the **forer unner** of CDP . (**Community Development Programme**)

Nilokheri Project:- Nilokheri Project was started by **S.K. Dey** design to rehabilitate about 7000 displaced person (immigrants) from Pakistan after partition . He began this project using 100 acre of swampy land spreading in the midst of Karnal and Kurukshetra. The colony had its own dairy, poultry,piggery,printing press, engineering workshop ,bone meal factory all run on cooperative lines. The Scheme was called *"Mazdoor Manzil"* because it was based on the principle of 'he who would not work neither shall he eat.

References:-

1. Mondal, S. (2019). Fundamentals of Agricultural Extension Education.New Delhi, Kalyani publishers.
2. O.P. Dhama and O.P. Bhatnagar (2006).Education and Communication for Development, , New Delhi:Oxford and IBH Publishing Co.
3. Ray GL (1996) Extension Communication and Management, Calcutta, West Bengal: Naya Prakash Publications.

CHAPTER FIVE

VARIOUS EXTENSION / AGRICULTURE DEVELOPMENT PROGRAMMES LAUNCHED BY ICAR / GOVT. OF INDIA

India has become self-sufficient in agriculture through increasing food production by many folds after green revolution. It was an integrated effort of the policy, research and extension support. Agriculture development in India is very location specific. However the Union Government play a guiding role in formulating policies to accelerate growth of agricultural sector. The programmes conceived at national level are mainly implemented by the various departments of state government. Indian Council of Agricultural Research (ICAR) is an apex body at the national level that supports research and extension activities to evolve effective Transfer of Technology (TOT) models. The State Agricultural Universities also contemplates to develop extension models suitable to take up transfer of technology besides implementing the models evolved by ICAR system. (K. Narayana Gowda).

There are many agricultural development and extension programmes which were launched by Government of India and ICAR. Some of them are listed below for a glance to understand their objectives and features. Among these programmes some are mentioned as "Programmes for technological Development" like IADP, IAAP, ICDP and HYVP, where as some are refereed as "Development programmes with Social Justice" viz MFAL, DPAP, T&V, IRDP, TRYSEM, NREP, DWACRA, NAEP, TMO, JRY, EAS, SFAC and SGSY. Later on various programmes were designed for "Infrastructure Development" like NATP, PURA, NAIP, NREGA and NFSM. Realizing the importance of changing climate and for resource conservation programmes like NICRA and FFS and SHC have been incorporated in the last decade. On a keen observation it is realized that every new programme was designed to fill the deficiency of previous programmes and experiences. Hence these programmes looks like quite related to each other and sometimes overlapping too. However they are capable to address every section of rural community in general and farming community in particular. Programmes introduced in 21st century involves ICT component to ensure faster delivery of information.

		Agricultural Development Programmes		
1	**IADP**	Intensive Agricultural District Programme	1960-61	Package programme, to increased agricultural productivity that lead to economic growth
2	**IAAP**	Intensive Agricultural Area Programme	1964	Extend the benefit of improved tech. in agri. in large areas at less cost and reduced staff strength
3	**HYVP**	High Yielding Varieties Programme	1964-65	Highly input intensive, attained self sufficiency sopped import grain resulting green revolution
4	**I V L P**	Institution Village Linkage Programme	1995-96	Based on scientist farmer participatory mode tech. intervention in small prod. System
5	**ORP**	Operational Research Project	1974	To test performance of new research on farmers field on operational level under their existing recourses
6	**N A T P**	National Agriculture Technology Project	1998	Location specific, demand driven TOT to farmers with research.– extn. – farmers - linkages
7	**NAIP**	National Agricultural innovation Project	2006	Promote research in the prod. To consumption mode, provide livelihood security in selected disadvantages regions,
8	**RKVY**	Rastriy Krishi Vikas Yojana	2007	Provide incentive to the state to achieve 4%groeth rate in agril. & allied sector in 11 plan

1. *Intensive Agricultural District Programme (IADP):-*

- It was felt that the increase in agriculture production under the community development programme was for less than necessary to feed the rapidly increasing population of this country.
- To tackle this urgent problem the government in collaboration with Ford Foundation launched the intensive agricultural district programme (1960-61) which is popularly known as the package programme.
- The significant feature of this programme is that the cooperative institutions have become the agency for distribution of credit and supply of agricultural inputs which were essential for

implementing the programme.

- The district selected throughout the country under this programme are pali, thanjavur, West-Godavari, Shahabad, Raipur, Aligarh, Ludhiana, Aleppey, palght, Mandga, Surat, Sambalpur, Bardwan, Bhandeva and Cochar.

Objectives:

1. To increase the income of the cultivator and his family.
2. To increase the economic resources and potential of the village.
3. To create employment facilities.
4. To demonstrate the most effective ways of expansion of the national food production technology by co-operative efforts between officials and not-officials, villagers and individual cultivators.

Criteria for selection of the district for IADP:

1. Districts have adequate supply of water.
2. Should have minimum natural hazards.
3. They have well developed village industry.
4. They have maximum potential to increase agricultural and animal production

The Distinctive features of IADP :-

1. To provide factors of production simultaneously, timely and adequately
2. Essential inputs like fertilizers, etc. to be made available 100 per cent of the requirement.
3. Credit to be provided to any farmer who joins the programme and has the potentials of the requirement.
4. More agricultural and cooperative staff to be posted
5. Provision of composite demonstrations instead of single factor demonstrations.

6. Periodical training of staff.
7. Analysis and evaluation.

The various activities under taken by IADP were:

1. Adequate and timely supply of credit and inputs (seed and fertilizers etc)
2. Provision of services such as market, storage and transport.
3. Emphasis on food and cash crops, livestock etc
4. Strengthening of cooperatives and panchayats.

Above efforts were made sincerely, but IADP suffered from the following limitations
Limitations:-

1. Educational approach to reach the cultivators was lacking
2. Poor trainings to staff
3. Staff was not clear about the methods of reaching the cultivators.
4. Posting of staff was not adequate
5. Workshop, seed testing and soil testing laboratories were not functioning to the required level
6. Transport and land development programmes were not progressing satisfactory

2. Intensive Agricultural Area Programme (IAAP)

Intensive Agriculture Area programme (IAAP) was launched in 1964-65. The core philosophy of the IAAP was that *"much greater emphasis should be given to the development of scientific and progressive agriculture in an intensive manner in the areas which have High production potentials"*. The idea was to cover at least 20% of the cultivated area of the country. The emphasis was on import crops such as Wheat, Rice, Millets, Cotton, Sugarcane, Potato, Pulses etc. The Intensive Agriculture Area programme (IAAP) paved the way for Green Revolution in the country.

3. High Yielding Varieties Programme (HYVP)

1. HYVP is launched in 1966, which helped the country in attaining self-sufficiency in food.
2. The technological development did not remain confined to the introduction of high yielding crop varieties alone.
3. These were combined with the application of high analysis and balanced fertilizer, irrigation, plant protection, improved implements etc, which made a 'green revolution' possible in the country.
4. The pervasive influence of high yielding technology spread to other areas of farm production such as animal production, such as animal production, fishery, sericulture, social forestry etc. Punjab, Haryana and Western parts of UP were initially selected for the phased launching of this strategy.
5. The cultivation of HYV since 1966-67 had resulted in a substantial increase in food grains production. Wheat production was doubled. Rice production also had a substantial increase, though not as much as in the case of wheat.
6. The target of coverage of 2.5 crore hectares of area under HYVs of cereals and millets under fourth five year plan was exceeded. The coverage was more than four crore hectares

4. Institution-Village Linkage Programme (IVLP):-

1. It is an innovative programme initiated by the Indian council of Agricultural Research (ICRA) on a pilot basis form 1995-96.
2. To help scientists to have direct interaction with the farming community so that appropriate technologies are developed for farmers.
3. Here research, extension and farmers establish firm links by carrying together the assessment and refinement functions in the technology development and dissemination process.
4. This helps the research system to generate a cafeteria of technologies, which are more productive in small production system, more profitable in commercial production system and gender sensitive for removal of drudgery of farm women.

5. Operational Research Project (ORP):-

ORP was initiated in 1975 to identify technological as well as socio-economic constraints and to formulate and implement a combination of technology modules on area/watershed/target group basis.

The performance of the new technology is to be tested on farmers" fields at operational level under the existing resources and socio-economic and cultural conditions to address the common agricultural problems affecting the existing farm production system on community basis.

6. National Agricultural Technology Project (NATP):-

1. This project was launched by the ICAR 30th June, 1998 with a support of World Bank to strengthen & complement the existing resources.
2. N A T P was the world biggest World Bank assisted agriculture project.

7. Agricultural Technology Management Agency (ATMA)

1. ATMA is a society of key stake holders engage in agricultural activities for sustainable agricultural developmental in the district
2. The registered office of ATMA is located in the premises of district collector.
3. A Centrally sponsored scheme 'Support to State Extension Programmes for Extension Reforms' was launched by the ICAR in 1999.
4. This scheme is a major initiative towards revitalizing agricultural extension in the States to make the extension system decentralized and demand driven.
5. ATMA is managed by Project Director at district level.

6. Agricultural Technology Information Centre (ATIC)

The Agricultural Technology Information Centre (ATIC) is a "single window" support system linking the various units of a research institution with intermediary users and end users (farmers) in decision making and problem solving exercise.

Agricultural Technology Information Centre are started in 1998-99 under NATP, sponsored by World Bank & implemented through more than forty ICAR & SAUs.

7. National Agricultural Innovation Project (NAIP):-

The Government of India has launched the National Agricultural Innovation project with a credit support of the World Bank. The project will run up to June 2012. The ICAR is operating the Project.

The overall objective of the project is to facilitate accelerated and sustainable transformation of Indian agriculture for rural poverty alleviation and income generation by the application of agricultural innovations through collaboration among public research organizations, farmers' groups, NGOs, the private sector and the civil societies and other stakeholders.

The India National Agricultural Innovation Project contributes to the sustainable transformation of Indian agricultural sector to more of a market orientation to relieve poverty and improve income.

The specific aim is to accelerate collaboration among public research organizations, farmers, the private sector and stakeholders in using agricultural innovations.

8. Rashtriya Krishi Vikas Yojana (RKVY):-

Rashtriya Krishi Vikas Yojana is a special Additional Central Assistance Scheme which was launched in August 2007 to orient agricultural development strategies, to reaffirm its commitment to achieve 4 per cent annual growth in the agricultural sector during the 11th plan. The scheme was launched to incentivize the States to provide additional resources in their State Plans over and above their baseline expenditure to bridge critical gaps.

CHAPTER SIX

NEW TRENDS IN AGRICULTURE EXTENSION

Privatization of Extension

Privatization broadly refers to a process by which the government reduces its role in an activity and encourages private sector to take up these roles.

Concept and Definition:

- ChandraShekara, 2001: The Process of funding and delivering the extension services by private individual or organization is called Private Extension.
- Bloom indicated that private sector extension involves personnel in the private sector extension involves personnel in the private sector.
- Vanden Ban and Hawkins (1996) state that in private sector extension, farmers are expected to share the responsibility for the service and pay all or part of the cost.

- Saravanan and ShivalingeGowda (1999) operationalized Privatization as follows: "Privatization of extension service refers to the services rendered in the area of agriculture and allied aspects by extension personnel working in private agencies or organizations for which farmers are expected to pay a fee (or free) and it can be viewed as supplementary or alternative to public extension services".

These concepts about the privatization emphasize three aspects:

- It involves extension personnel from private agency/ organization.

- Clients are expected to pay the service fee.

- Act as supplementary or alternative to public extension service.

Through the process of privatization, extension effectiveness is expected to improve by:

- reorienting public sector extension with limited and well-focused functions, more number of extension providers (institutional pluralism) resulting from active encouragement by the public sector to initiate, operate and expand.
- more private participation leading to the availability of specialized services hitherto not available from the public system
- user contributions to extension leading to improved financial sustainability, Support and control by clients leading to client orientation Reasons behind privatization of extension services.

Privatization can take place broadly in two ways:

- Dismantling of Public sector

  - Controlled Privatization

Following are some of the reasons behind privatization in agricultural extension services:

1. Fiscal crisis: Many less developed country's governments have found it difficult to make adequate resources available for extension. Financial pressures have, in turn led to the search for ways of reduction in public sector costs.
2. Disappointing performance of public extension system: Impact of public extension system in agricultural development is disappointing. Extension work is ineffective, does not match with farmer's needs, there is little

consideration for cost-effectiveness and less competent extension personnel have no accountability to farmers. Moreover, public extension alone will never answer to entire demand of farming community.

1. Changing contexts and opportunities: In recent past Indian agriculture is shifting from mere subsistence level to commercialized agribusiness to meet all challenges and opportunities of globalization and liberalization, effective alternative extension approach is required. Increasing commercial and specialized nature of agriculture will demand quickly and technically sound advice, based on scientific analysis with appropriate marketing information. Further India is facing population explosion which had resulted into reduction in land holding size.

Due to improved transport network and better communication facilities private agencies and communication media are also reaching to remote villages.

Therefore, there is an urgent need for an efficient technological guidance along with recent market information, which is only possible through privatization of extension services.

4. The extension worker: the extension worker and farmers ratio is very wide in India i.e. 1:1000 and it is further widens due to engagement of extension workers in administrative work, official correspondence, report etc.

Advantages of Private Extension System (Sulaiman and Sadamate , 2000):

1. Reorienting public sector extension with limited and well focussed functions. More number of extension providers (institutional pluralism) resulting from active encouragement by the public sector to initiate, operate and expand.
2. More private participation leading to the availability of specialized services hitherto not available from the public system.
3. Support and control by clients leading to client orientation.

Disadvantages of Private Extension System (Vanden Ban and Hawkins, 1998):

1. Privatization may hamper free flow of information.
2. Farmers may be less interested to disseminate technologies to other farmers what they have learnt from private extension.
3. Only commercial farmers will be benefited through privatization and subsistence farmers will seldom be able to pay the fee.
4. The commercial interest of the private agencies may jeopardize the efforts of research and extension of eco-friendly and sustainable agriculture.

5. Contact between farmers and extension agents get declined.

Reference:

1. De, D. and Jirli, B. (2010). A Handbook of Extension Education. Jodhpur, Agrobios (India).
2. Govind, S., Tamilselvi, G. and Meenambigai, J. (2011). Extension Education and Rural Development, Jodhpur, Agrobios (India).
3. Joy, D. and Sreekumar, K. (2014). A Survey of Expert System in Agriculture. *International Journal of Computer Science and Information Technologies*, 5 (6): 7861-7864.
4. Mishra, S. and Akankasha. 2014. Expert Systems In Agriculture: An overview. *International Journal of Science Technology & Engineering*, 1(5): 45-49.
5. Mondal, S. (2018). Communication Skills and Personality Development, Entrepreneurship Development and Business Communication. New Delhi, Kalyani publishers.
6. Mondal, S. (2019). Fundamentals of Agricultural Extension Education. New Delhi. Kalyani publishers,
7. Sulaiman, V.R. and Sadamate, V.V. (2000) 'Privatising agricultural extension in India', Policy Paper 10. New Delhi: National Centre for Agricultural Economics and Policy Research.
8. The Computer Revolution/Artificial Intelligence/Expert Systems. Retrieved from https://en.m.wikibooks.org/wiki/ The_Computer_Revolution/Artificial_Intelligen ce/Expert_Sys tems

CHAPTER SEVEN

CYBER EXTENSION/ E-EXTENSION

Cyber

According to Oxford dictionary the word Cyber means "relating to Information technology, the Internet and virtual reality, the Cyber space. The word has its origin from cybernetics.

Cyber space

The cyber space is the imaginary or virtual space of computer connected with each other on networks, across the globe. These computers can access information in form of text, graphics, audio, video and animation files. Software tools on network provide facilities to interactively access the information from connected services. The cyber space thus can be defined as the imaginary space behind the interconnected telecommunications and computer networks, the virtual world.

Extension

Extension stands for "the action or process of enlarging or extending something". It could be extension of area, time or space.

E-extension and cyber extension are more or less synonymous and can be used interchangeably. Cyber extension and e-extension are extension approaches; whereas ICT is the tools by which various services are delivered to the clientele fulfilling the objectives of e-extension/ cyber extension (Mondal, 2019).

Cyber extension

According to Sharma (2005) Cyber extension can be defined as the "Extension over cyber space". Cyber extension means "using the power of online networks, computer communications and digital interactive multimedia to facilitate dissemination of agricultural technology". Cyber extension includes effective use of information and communication technology, national and international information networks, internet, expert system, multimedia learning systems and computer based training systems to improve information access to the farmers, extension workers, research scientists and extension managers.

Cyber agricultural extension is an agricultural information exchange mechanism over cyber space, the imaginary space behind the interconnected computer networks through telecommunication means. It utilizes the power of networks, computer communications and interactive multimedia to facilitate information sharing mechanism (Wijekoon, 2003).

IT and ICT

IT (Information Technology) refers to computer based technology and telecommunications.IT refers to an entire industry that uses computers, networking, software and other equipment to manage information. Generally, IT departments are responsible for storing, processing, transmitting, retrieving and protecting digital information of the company.

ICT (Information Communications Technology) can be seen as an integration of IT with mediation broadcasting technologies, audio/ video processing and transmission and telephony. Therefore, ICT can be seen as an extended acronym for IT.

ICTs are those technologies that can be used to interlink information technology devices such as personal computers with communication technologies such as telephones and their telecommunication networks. The PC, laptop and tablet with e-mail and internet provides the best example (Mondal, 2019).

Information provided through Cyber extension

Cyber extension can provide large amount of information to farmers. Some of those as mentioned by Sharma are:

1. ***Weather:*** Daily information of maximum and minimum temperature, day length, direction and speed of wind, rain fall, relative humidity and weather forecasting.
2. ***Alert:*** Information regarding type of disaster, sudden change in weather, outbreak of diseases and insects etc.
3. ***Insurance:*** Detail information about insurance of farmers, his crop, animal and agricultural assets like tractors, implements and tools etc.
4. **General awareness:** Information about vaccination, cleanliness, health, family planningand nutrition.
5. ***Rural Finance:*** Information about micro finance and subsidy etc.
6. ***Education:*** Detail information about farmers training and educational knowledge of his children about professional and non-professional institution.
7. ***Animal Science:*** The detail regarding the local animal and well known diseases, better breeds, balanced feed, shed management, health etc.

Advantages of Cyber Extension

1. Information can be provided quickly to farmers.
2. Round the clock service to farmers.
3. Information can be accessed from any place on the earth.
4. Helpful in enhancing the communication efficiency.
5. Preserves the quality of message.
6. Experts can be contacted directly.
7. Per unit cost is less as compared to traditional system of extension.

Limitation of cyber extension

1. Lack of reliable telecom infrastructure in ruralareas.
2. Erratic or no power supply.
3. Lack of ICT trained manpower (willing to serve) in rural areas.

4. Lack of content (locally relevant and in local language).
5. Low purchasing power of rural people.
6. Lack of holistic approach.
7. Issues of sustainability.

Reference:

1. De, D. and Jirli, B. (2010). A Handbook of Extension Education. Jodhpur, Agrobios (India).
2. Govind, S., Tamilselvi, G. and Meenambigai, J. (2011). Extension Education and Rural Development, Jodhpur, Agrobios (India).
3. Joy, D. and Sreekumar, K. (2014). A Survey of Expert System in Agriculture. *International Journal of Computer Science and Information Technologies*, 5 (6): 7861-7864.
4. Mishra, S. and Akankasha. 2014. Expert Systems In Agriculture: An overview. *International Journal of Science Technology & Engineering*, 1(5): 45-49.
5. Mondal, S. (2018). Communication Skills and Personality Development, Entrepreneurship Development and Business Communication. New Delhi, Kalyani publishers.
6. Mondal, S. (2019). Fundamentals of Agricultural Extension Education. New Delhi. Kalyani publishers,

CHAPTER EIGHT

FARMER-LED EXTENSION

The present day agriculture is defined by key concept of stability, sustainability, diversification and commercialization. In the last decade, the agricultural situation in India had undergone a tremendous change in the light of liberation and establishment of World Trade Organization (WTO). India's signing of General Agreement on Trade and Tariff (GATT) in 1914 and joining of WTO has put our agriculture into a frame work of global market. Low productivity of crops added to less remunerative market prices of agricultural commodities are the major causes of worry. Thus, agricultural enterprise is found to be not very profitable although a large majority is depending on it. With the globalization of agriculture, major emphasis has been given on Production- led Extension.

Initially in India, through main thrust for development was laid on Agriculture, communication, education, industry, health and allied sector but later on it was realized that accelerated development can be provided only if governmental efforts are adequately supplemented by direct and indirect involvement of people at the gross root level.

Over time, extension provision has been supply- driven, with little direct consultation with the farmers to whom the extension technologies, information and associated services are intended. The linear model of technology transfer (researcher- extension-farmers) has been the dominant approach to agriculture and rural development, resulting in the delivery of technologies that have failed to alleviate farmers' problems. Clearly, more locally controlled organizations, governments and donors throughout Asia, Africa and Latin America have been experimenting with a range of approaches to extension. These include the campesino-a-campasino movement of Central America, Farmers field schools in Southeast Asia, problem census approaches in South Asia and information facilitation progrmame in Africa.

Recently, farmer –led-extension approaches have come to be considered as appropriate for framers need. These approaches increase farmer's basic knowledge and ability to make their own choices and decision on particular technologies. Farmers assume a central role and become key players in technology identification, generation, adaptation and dissemination.

Farmers innovate due to necessity, to changing conditions and also simply as a result of curiosity. Innovations result from doing informal experiments on new ideas either from their own ingenuity or learned from other farmers, researchers, extensionists and other information sources like the mass media. However, research and extension normally pay little attention to the importance of local innovation for agricultural development.

The farmer led extension approach gives farmers the opportunity to share their experiences and practices through a method demo with fellow farmers in the area. It was noted that farmers who were successful in their farming venture have established credibility among their peers. In selecting the farmer extensionist, the primary consideration is- he should be an innovative farmer, active and hardworking, honest and credible interested in learning, accepted and committed to the community, and most importantly interested to share his knowledge and skills. Likewise a farmer extensionist must have conducted a techno demo trial and field day, preferably attended the FFS. He must also have the capacity and willingness to finance the cost of technology.

Farmer-to-Farmer extension is defined here as "the provision of training by farmers to farmers, often through the creation of a structure of farmer promoters and farmer trainers.

Meaning of Farmer Led Extension (FLE)

Farmer Led Extension is promising approach where in farmer leaders were utilized as extensionists to transfer the technologies they learned with a view to boost up the production. The FLE approach gives farmers the opportunity to share their experiences and practices through a method demonstration with fellow framers in the area.

Concepts of FLE:

1. Farm Schools
2. Farmer Field Schools

Farm School: Farm school is a field where latest technology was demonstrated to progressive and interested farmers who undergo training for a certain period of time. Farm schools help in speedy dissemination and adoption of technologies through training of progressive farmers on the latest production technology.

The farm school was established by E. I. D. Parry and Co. near their sugar factory at Nellikuppam, South Arcot district of Tamilnadu.

Farmers Field Schools:

- Farmer Field School (FFS) is non-formal educational activity.
- All learning is a group activity and field based.
- Empowers farmers to solve their field problems by themselves.
- Fosters participation, interaction and joint decision making.
- Farmers learn by carrying out activities through constant observation
- The Farmer Field School is a form of adult education, which evolved from the concept that farmers learn optimally from field observation and experimentation.

- It was developed to help farmers tailor their Integrated Pest Management (IPM) practices to diverse and dynamic ecological conditions
- In regular sessions from planting till harvest, groups of neighboring farmers observe and discuss dynamics of the crop's ecosystem. Simple experimentation helps farmers further improve their understanding of functional relationships (e.g. pests-natural enemy population dynamics and crop damage-yield relationships). In this cyclical learning process, farmers develop the expertise that enables them to make their own crop management decisions. Special group activities encourage learning from peers, and strengthen communicative skills and group building.
- IPM Farmer Field Schools were started in 1989 in Indonesia to reduce farmer reliance on pesticides in rice.
- Policy-makers and donors were impressed with the results and the program rapidly expanded.
- Follow-up training activities were added to enhance community-based activities and local program ownership. Eventually, IPM Farmer Field School programs for rice were carried out in twelve Asian countries and gradually branched out to vegetables, cotton and other crops.
- From the mid-nineties onwards, the experience generated in Asia was used to help initiate IPM Farmer Field School programs in other parts of the world.
- New commodities were added and local adaptation and institutionalization of these programs was encouraged.
- At present, IPM Farmer Field School programs, at various levels of development, are being conducted in over 30 countries world wide
- These diverse programs have generated a variety of data on the impact of the IPM Farmer Field School.
- Such data generally are presented in project reports that have a limited circulation.

- Impact studies that are published in official literature tend to focus on specific aspects of impact.
- Impact studies varied in focus, approach, methodology and robustness. Some lack description of methods.
- The nature of impact studies typically varies with the developmental stages of programs.
- Pilot projects often compared pesticide use and yields or profits of field plots grown with IPM practices and those under regular farmer practice, to demonstrate the merit of the approach.
- More advanced projects evaluated the adoption of IPM practices, studied expertise or recorded the developmental impacts resulting from farmer empowerment.

There are 5 types of farmers-led extension:

1. Farmers to farmer
2. Farmer field school

3. The problem census

4. Problem solving approach

5. NGO government collaboration

Paradigm shift from production-led to farmers-led extension system (Kokate et al., 2009)

Components	Production-led	Farmers- led
Purpose/ Objective	Transfer of productiontechnologies	Capacity building (especially farmers extensionist), create para-professional technologies extension workers, creating or strengthening local Institutions
Goal	Food self-sufficiency	Livelihood security including food, nutrition, employment to alleviate poverty Sustainability and conserving bio- Diversity
Approach	Top-down, commo dity and supply driven	Participatory, bottom-up anddemand Driven
Actors	Mostly publicinstitutions	Pluralistic with public, private,non- government and farmers organizations as a partner rather than competitors
Mode	Mostly interpersonal/ individual approach	Integration of clients oriented on-farm participatory/ experiential learning methodssupported by ICTs and media
Role of Extension agents	Limited to delivery mode and feedback to research system	Facilitation of learning, buildingoverall capacity of farmers an encouraging farmersexperimentation
Linkages/liaison	Research-Extension Farmers	Research-Extension-Farmers Organizations (FIGs, CIGs,SHGs)
Emphasis	Information management, Production "Seed to Seed"	Knowledge management and sharing
Nature of technology	Input intensive, cropbased and general recommendations as per agro-climatic zone, fixed package of information	Knowledge intensive, broad based, farming systemperspective and blending with ITKs
Critical areas	Improvement, production and protection	Decision support system, integrated farming system approach, natural resourcemanagement, client group formation and community Empowerment
Critical inputs	Money and material	Access to information, buildinghuman and social capital
Accountability	Mostly government	To farmers rather than donors

Reference:

1. De, D. and Jirli, B. (2010). A Handbook of Extension Education. Jodhpur, Agrobios (India).
2. Govind, S., Tamilselvi, G. and Meenambigai, J. (2011). Extension Education and Rural Development, Jodhpur, Agrobios (India).
3. Joy, D. and Sreekumar, K. (2014). A Survey of Expert System in Agriculture. *International Journal of Computer Science and Information Technologies*, 5 (6): 7861-7864.
4. Mishra, S. and Akankasha. 2014. Expert Systems In Agriculture: An overview. *International Journal of Science Technology & Engineering*, 1(5): 45-49.

CHAPTER NINE

RURAL DEVELOPMENT

Rural development has always been an important issue in all discussions pertaining to economic development, especially of developing countries, throughout the world. In the developing countries and some formerly communist societies, rural mass comprise a substantial majority of the population. Over 3.5 billion people live in the Asia and Pacific region and some 63% of them in rural areas. Although millions of rural people have escaped poverty as a result of rural development in many Asian countries, a large majority of rural people continue to suffer from persistent poverty. The socio-economic disparities between rural and urban areas are widening and creating tremendous pressure on the social and economic fabric of many developing Asian economies. These factors, among many others, tend to highlight the importance of rural development. The policy makers in most of the developing economies recognize this importance and have been implementing a host of programs and measures to achieve rural development objectives. While some of these countries have achieved impressive results, others have failed to make a significant dent in the problem of persistent rural under development.

Rural - Is an area, where the people are engaged in primary industry in the sense that they produce things directly for the first time in cooperation with nature as stated by Srivastava (1961).

Rural Areas - Rural areas are sparsely settled places away from the influence of large cities and towns. Such areas are distinct from more intensively settled urban and suburban areas, and also from unsettled lands such as outback or wilderness. People live in village, on farms and in other isolated houses. Rural areas can have an agricultural character, though many rural areas are characterized by an economy based on logging, mining, oil and gas exploration, or tourism.

Lifestyles - Lifestyles in rural areas are different than those in urban areas, mainly because limited services are available. Governmental services like law enforcement, schools, fire departments, and libraries may be distant, limited in scope, or unavailable. Utilities like water, sewer, street lighting, and garbage collection may not be present. Public transport is sometimes absent or very limited; people use their own vehicles, walk or ride an animal.

A society or community can be classified as rural based on the criteria of lower population density, less social differentiation, less social and spatial mobility, slow rate of social change, etc. Agriculture would be the major occupation of rural area.

Development - It refers to growth, evolution, stage of inducement or progress. This progress or growth is gradual and had sequential phases. Always there is increasing differentiation. It also refers to the overall movement towards greater efficiency and complex situations.

Rural Development (RD) is a process, which aims at improving the well-being and self-realization of people living outside the urbanized areas through collective process.

According to Agarwal (1989), rural development is a strategy designed to improve the economic and social life of rural poor.

Scope and Importance of Rural Development

Rural development is a dynamic process, which is mainly concerned with the rural areas. These include agricultural growth, putting up of economic and social infrastructure, fair wages as also housing and house sites for the landless, village planning, public health, education and functional literacy, communication etc.

Rural development is a national necessity and has considerable importance in India because of the following reasons.

1. About three-fourth of India's population live in rural areas, thus rural development is needed to develop nation as whole.
2. Nearly half of the country's national income is derived from agriculture, which is major occupation of rural India.
3. Around seventy per cent of Indian population gets employment through agriculture.
4. Bulks of raw materials for industries come from agriculture and rural sector.
5. Increase in industrial population can be justified only in rural population"s motivation andincreasing the purchasing power to buy industrial goods.
6. Growing disparity between the urban elite and the rural poor can lead to political instability.

The main objective of the rural development programme is to raise the economic and social level of the rural people.

The specific objectives are:

1. To develop farm, home, public service and village community.
2. To bring improvement in producing of crops and animals living condition.
3. To improve health and education condition etc. improvement of the rural people.
4. To improve villagers with their own efforts.
5. To improve village communication.

Problems in Rural Development
1. People related:

*   Traditional way of thinking.
*   Poor understanding.

- Low level of education to understand developmental efforts and new technology.
- Deprived psychology and scientific orientation.
- Lack of confidence.
- Poor awareness.
- Low level of education.
- Existence of unfelt needs.
- Personal ego.

2. Agricultural related problems:

- Lack of expected awareness, knowledge, skill and attitude.
- Unavailability of inputs.
- Poor marketing facility.
- Insufficient extension staff and services.
- Multidimensional tasks to extension personnel.
- Small size of land holding.
- Division of land.
- Unwillingness to work and stay in rural areas.

3. Infrastructure related problems:

Poor infrastructure facilities like water, electricity, transport, educational communication, health, storage facility etc.

4. Economic problems:

- Unfavorable economic condition to adopt high cost technology.
- High cost of inputs.
- Underprivileged rural industries

5. Social and Cultural problems:

- Cultural norms and traditions
- Conflict within and between groups, castes, religions, regions, languages.

1. **Leadership related problems:**

   1. Leadership among the hands of inactive and incompetent people.
   2. Malafied interest of leaders.
   3. Biased political will.
   4. Administrative problems:
   5. Earlier, majority of the programmes were planning based on top to bottom approach and were target oriented.
   6. Political interference.
   7. Lack of motivation and interest.
   8. Unwillingness to work in rural area.
   9. Improper utilization of budget.

References

1. De, D. and Jirli, B. (2010). A Handbook of Extension Education. Agrobios (India), Jodhpur.
2. Mondal, S. (2019). Fundamentals of Agricultural Extension Education. Kalyani publishers, New Delhi.

CHAPTER TEN

RURAL LEADERSHIP: CONCEPT AND DEFINITION, TYPES OF LEADERS IN RURAL CONTEXT

It is difficult for any country to provide enough number of extension workers to reach each and every family for its development programmes. It is rather more difficult for the developing countries where the resources are scarce. This problem can be solved to some extent through the use of local leaders.

A local leader who has adopted improved practices extends the same to others. The common man has much faith in local leaders. A villager would like to hear and imitate his own neighbor as compared to accepting the advices of an outside change agent. Moreover there is a healthy competition among the villagers which promotes action among them.

There is no doubt that extension worker also has to play the role of leader but he may confine his role to the few selected contact farmers. The information from the extension workers will reach these leader farmers which will further trickle down to other people from the leader farmers. These leaders would like to act as local leaders and feel pleasure in serving to others. They must have certain qualities. He should be a person from the same community and has the same type of resources. It has been often observed that innovators and big farmers do not pass on freely their knowledge to other people in the village due to some gap. It is, therefore, essential for the students of extension education to study the process of leadership. Once the process of dissemination through leaders is known the introduction of new ideas through village leaders can be solved to a great extent.

Leader

1. Leader is a person who has been spontaneously considered or chosen as being influential. - **Dahama & Bhatnagar**
2. Leader is the servant of the group. The position of leader is an essential mechanism of effective group organization. - **Sanderson**
3. Leaders are persons who are selected by the people because of their special interest or fitness to work on several phases of the local programmes. - **J. S. Gang**
4. A leader is one who, in a social situation, can elicit (stimulate) positive reaction from other members of the group. - **B.M.Stogdill**

Leadership

According to Niderfrank (1966) leadership is essential in simply influencing attitudes and actions of one or more persons leading towards the achievement or so purpose.

"Leadership is an act that influences" says **Tead (1926)**.

Cartwright and Zender (1960) perceived leadership as the performance of all that help the group to achieve its preferred outcome.

Lester (1975) defines leadership as the resource that an individual or group USI to enable the organization to do what it needs, should or wants to do.

According to Davis (1977) "Leadership is the ability to persuade others to seek defined objectives enthusiastically".

Dahama and Bhatnagar (1985), leadership is the process who in any social situation with his ideas and actions influence the thoughts and behaviour of other Leadership are the process of influencing the thoughts and behaviour of others towards goal setting and goal achievement.

Functions of Leaders

There is no unanimity of opinion as to what the functions of leadership are. Generally speaking leadership functions are related to goal achievement and to the maintenance and strengthening of the group.

According to Barnard, a leader performs four main functions. They are:

- Determination of objective
- Manipulation of means
- Control of the instrumentality of action; and
- Stimulation of coordination action.

According to Dahama and Bhatnagar (1985) following are the functions:

- Executive
- Planner
- Policy maker
- Expert in human relations as well as technical field.
- External group representative
- Controller of internal relationship
- Purveyor of reward and punishment
- Arbitrator
- Exemplar
- Group symbol
- Surrogate of individual responsibility
- Idealist

- Father figure and
- Scape goat

Classification of Leaders

Different authors classified the leaders in different ways. Some of the classifications are:

1. **Beal, Bohlen and Raudabaugh (1962)** classified the leaders into four types as;

   a. Born leaders
   b. Passive leaders (personal power or characteristic leader)
   c. Bureaucratic leaders and
   d. Democratic leaders

2. **Mott (1972)** spoke about three major leadership categories

   a. Democratic
   b. Multifactor and
   c. Situational

3. **Henning (1962)** analyzed the leadership and given the following three:

   a. Autocrat
   b. Bureaucrat and
   c. Neurocrat

4. **Lester (1975)** also pointed three types as:

   a. Autocratic
   b. Democratic and
   c. Free rein

5. **Haiman (1951)** described five categories as the

a. Executive
b. Judge
c. Advocate
d. Expert and
e. Discussion leader

6. **Carter (1961)** identified three leadership patterns according to the manner in which the leader was mostly oriented. They are,

   a. Personal

   b. Institutional and
   c. Flexible

8. **Sachdeva and Vidyabhushan (1974)** studied three main leadership types as;

   a. Authoritarian
   b. Democratic and
   c. Laissez-faire

9. **Dahama and Bhatnagar (1985)** found several ways of classifying leaders, some of them are;

   a. Democratic, autocratic and laissez-faire
   b. Formal and informal leaders
   c. Professional and lay (voluntary) leaders
   d. Political, religious, social and academic
   e. Elected, selected or nominated
   f. Popular and unpopular
   g. Traditional and progressive leaders

Characteristics of Leaders

The characteristics of leaders differ. The characteristics of three types of leaders are as detailed:

1. **Autocratic**

    a. Determines all policies, activities and goals of the organization.
    b. Takes no part in work except when conducting meeting, telling others what to do or demonstrating.
    c. Members are uncertain about what to do and usually take actions they are told to take.
    d. Leader is personal in both praise and criticism of the work.

2. **Democratic**

    a. Produces a shared leadership that permits a feeling of satisfaction and achievement.
    b. Helps the members of understand the steps required in working.
    c. Members take more responsibility for group maintenance and task performance.

4. **Laissez-faire**

    a. Gives minimum guidance
    b. Remains in the background and seldom express an opinion or works with a minimum of roles.
    c. Members often act as leaders in making decisions that guide the organization.

5. **Democratic leadership**

In extension education, the extension worker will be dealing mainly with democratic leadership. Therefore it will be worthwhile to know their advantages and limitations.

Advantages

- People fully understand those ideas which they have helped to formulate.
- Decision made by the group members will get more support from the members.
- Democratic leadership enables the society to grow upon all of' the human resources that are available to it.
- Democratic leadership creates strong, responsible and self-reliant individuals.
- It builds a group which will not fall apart if something happens to the leaders.
- Democratic leadership makes for higher morale in a society than does the autocratic leadership.
- Those who disagree with group decisions are free to express their discontent, even though they may have to abide by the group decisions.
- It is always opened to the possibility of change.
- The method of making social decisions is important as the decisions themselves.

Limitations

- The vocal and powerful members become dominant, thus creating sense of inequality in the group.
- Policies are agreed upon verbally in groups which do not automatically provide an answer to every specific question which arises.
- Problem of individual who refuses to confirm to group decisions.
- Decision making is a time consuming process. The officials have to face the tyranny of indecisions.
- Participation of large number of people becomes a problem, because the physical limit to the number of people who can work together conveniently at one time.

Quality of leaders

Dahama and Bhatnagar (1985) brought out the determinants of effectiveness in leadership functions (ten 'A's).

1. Awareness of the functions of the group.
2. Ability (self-adjustment) in performing the functions
3. Achievement of goals
4. Assignment of group functions to members
5. Appraisal of effects of distribution of functions
6. Accomplishment of different purposes under different environments
7. Attainment of positive value as a leader
8. Attaching a high code of conduct, ethical values and high morale in the group
9. Arrangement of communication structures
10. Acceptance of failure

They have also identified through researches the most important factors for effectiveness of leaders. The factors identified are given below:

1. Need fulfillment
2. Prestige
3. Valued membership
4. Co-operative relationship
5. Heightened interaction
6. Clarity of goal
7. Small units
8. Homogeneity
9. Outside events   **10.**Increased position   **11.**Attack from environment

Role of Leaders
Reddy (1987) brought out the following eight important roles.

1. **Group Spokesman :** Leader has the responsibility to speak for the group and representing the group's interests and position faithfully and accurately.

2. **Group Harmonizer:** All groups will usually have both uniformities and differences of opinion. The leader is responsible for pointing out to the group when potential conflict situations arise, that the common purpose is sufficiently worthy of co-operation that the differences be resolved peacefully.

3. **Group Planner:** Generally persons are chosen for leadership positions because it is assumed that they know a little more about the problems confronting the group and their possible solutions than do the other members of the group. The group expects its leader to have new ideas for initiating activities. To meet this expectation leader must be able to plan, and visualize in his imagination, the ways by which the group can satisfy its needs.

4. **Group Executive:** Most groups have established some methods of conducting business and achieving consensus of opinion on issues that come up before them. The leader is one who presides when the group is conducting business. As a group executive the leader is responsible for seeing that the business of the organisation is carried on according to democratic principles.

5. **Group Educator or Teacher:** Leader must share with the followers' his knowledge and experience. Such sharing of experience and insight is teaching. Good leadership depends a large part upon because the good teacher is not a dictator.

6. **Symbol of Group:** Ideals All social groups have implicit or explicit norms or ideas. As a rule, persons accepted as leaders are those who have accepted these norms and live by them. The group expects his leadership to embody the ideals of group.

7. **Group Discussion Chairman:** This role is more related to that of group executive. In recent years there has been an increased interest in group discussions. Generally a group meets for a panel discussion or a forum or a group thinking conference as something apart from the routine business of the organization.

8. **Group Supervisor:** The leader has to work with followers and also with group organizations like youth clubs, co-operatives, farmer's associations, etc. Therefore this role becomes important for the leader.

References

1. De, D. and Jirli, B. (2010). A Handbook of Extension Education. Agrobios (India), Jodhpur.
2. Mondal, S. (2019). Fundamentals of Agricultural Extension Education. Kalyani publishers, New Delhi.
3. Adivi Reddy, A., 2001, *Extension Education*, Sree Lakshmi press, Bapatla.
4. Dahama, O. P. and Bhatnagar, O. P., 1998, *Education and Communication for Development*, Oxford and IBH publishing Co. Pvt. Ltd., New Delhi.
5. Jalihal, K. A. and Veerabhadraiah, V., 2007, *Fundamentals of Extension Education and Management in Extension*, Concept publishing company, New Delhi.
6. Muthaiah Manoraharan, P. and Arunachalam, R., *Agricultural Extension*, Himalaya Publishing House (Mumbai).
7. Rathore, O. S. *et al.*, 2012, *Handbook of Extension Education*, Agrotech Publishing Academy, Udaipur.

CHAPTER ELEVEN

EXTENSION ADMINISTRATION: MEANING AND CONCEPT, PRINCIPLES AND FUNCTIONS

Meaning of administration

The Management of public affairs of a government or institution is called administration. In extension education knowledge of administration is very important which can be developed by administrators. This knowledge will make the administrators aware of some of the unanticipated consequences of their decision. Secondly proper administration makes the administrator to his/her skill. Knowledge for solving problems of organization for which they are members.

Administration can be defined as the guidance leadership and control of the efforts of a group of individuals towards some common goal. According to this definition the essence of administration is the ability of administrator to plan large projects held together and organization for its accomplishment. Keep the organization functioning smoothly and efficiently and achieve the agreed upon objecting well within the allotment of the personal, time and resources available and without doing all the work himself.

Definition of Administration

Administration is the guidance, leadership and control of the efforts of a group of persons towards some common goals. Administration implies conscientious efforts directed towards organizing and controlling human activities in order to achieve agreed or desired goals. It involves, therefore, the organization, direction and control of persons and facilities in order to accomplish specified ends.

Administration involves essential activities of the people charged with ordering, forwarding and facilitating the efforts of individuals or groups brought together for desirable purposes. It involves efforts such as decision-making,

programming, communicating relevant information, controlling and evaluating various actions.

Administration is used during policy formulation for developing staff, understanding the planning process, job description, training and evaluation processes.

Management Versus Administration

- Management is a part of Administration. Management is an administrative technique in the conduct of public affairs. The traditional framework within which a civil service exercises its responsibilities is described as an administration.
- Administration lays emphasis on proper procedure, regulation and control. It employs ease of communication to achieve unambiguity – interpreting words and issues to ease the operation of a system.
- Administration takes place in the health sector, universities, army, church, agriculture, industries, business and social

organizations such as the Agricultural Extension Service.

Basic principles of administration

It is assumed that increased effectiveness of administration will occur when the principles of administration are followed. These principles are also called guidelines as they guide the administration in the performance of their job.

Principle of Hierarchy

- The members of the organizations are arranged in a definite subordinate – super ordinate hierarchy of line positions (eg Clas I, II, III and IV). It is also known as the 'Scalar process', where in lines of positional authority and responsibility run upward and downward through several levels with a broad base at the bottom and a single head at the top in order to preserve the 'unity of command'
- In the effective organization each worker knows who his supervisor is and each supervisor knows whom he is expected to supervise. If a worker is subject to orders from several supervisors (as in case of village development officer), he gets confused, in efficient and irresponsible. In this arrangement the authority of making vital decision is entrusted with a specialized person located at the helm of the organization.

Principles of Authority: Effective administration will occur when authority allocated to and individual or group of individuals is sufficient. The authority and the responsibility should be clearly defined and understand by all persons in the organizations. The different types of authorities are given in the following pages.

Principles of responsibility with matching authority: The individual should not be burdened only with responsibilities but should also be provided with matching authority. This is more important in a decentralized form of administration. Responsibility without authority is just lie leaving an individual to fight with a tiger without a gun or weapon.

Principles of span of control: Span of control is the number of subordinates one has he supervise. In general, the span of control is such as to permit to decision making as it needed. It helps in attaining quality decision. It results in increased effectiveness and efficiency in attaining the organizational objectives. Some of the factors influencing the span of control include

- the intensity and frequency of the need to see the chief,
- the age of the agency
- the magnitude of their problems
- the professional competence and length of service of the staff
- the size of the agency
- the size of the geographic area in which the supervisor must operate
- the importance of the decisions which the supervisor must make
- the degree of control that must be exercised
- the degree of repetitiveness of the work to be done.

Principles of communication: There should be two way channel of communication, both vertical and horizontal in the organization. Communication ensures common understanding of organization values and objectives clear and proper assignments of authority and functions are required for success in large operations. Employees want to know what is going on without a broad sharing of information and purpose their morale will be low and the agency's task will be more difficult.

Principles of organizational structure: The organization can no longer remain fixed or static changes in basic objectives, in size of staff, in professional competency, adjustments in programme emphasis, in the nature of institutional relationship within which the organization must operate will have to be made. Similarly the need for long range as well as short range planning of programmer personnel and finances may require many adjustments, in the form of the administrative organizational structures. In short the organizational structure should be subject to continues adaptations as conditions warrant.

Functions of administration

Administrators, broadly speaking, engage in a common set of functions to meet the organizations goals. These 'functions' of the administrator were described by 'Henri Fayol'as the '5 elements of administration'.

1. **Planning:** Planning is deciding in advances what to do, how to do it, when to do it and who should do it. It maps the path from where the organization is to, where it wants to be. The planning function involves establishing goals and arranging them in logical order. Administration engages in both short- range and long range planning.

2. **Organizing:** organizing involves identifying responsibilities to be performed, grouping responsibilities into departments or division and specifying organizational relationships. The purpose is to achieve coordinated efforts among all the elements in the organization. Organization must take into account delegation of authority and responsibility and span of control within supervisory units.

3. **Staffing:** staffing means filling job positions with the right at the right time. It involves determining staffing needs, writing job descriptions, recruiting and screening people to fill positions.

4. **Directing:** Directing in leading people in a manner that achieves the goals of the organization. This involves proper allocation of resources and providing an effective support. Directing requires exceptional interpersonal skills and the ability to motivate people. One of the crucial issues in directing is to find the correct balance between emphasis on staff needs and emphasis on economic production.

5. **Controlling:** Controlling is the function that evaluates quality in all areas and detects potential or actual deviations from the organization plan. This ensures high quality performance and satisfactory results while maintaining an orderly and problem free environment controlling includes information management

measurement of performance and institutions of correcting actions.

6. **Budgeting:** Exempted from the list above, incorporates most of the administrative functions, beginning with the implementation of a budget plan through the application of budget controls.

References

1. De, D. and Jirli, B. (2010). A Handbook of Extension Education. Agrobios (India), Jodhpur.
2. Mondal, S. (2019). Fundamentals of Agricultural Extension Education. Kalyani publishers, New Delhi.
3. Adivi Reddy, A., 2001, *Extension Education*, Sree Lakshmi press, Bapatla.
4. Dahama, O. P. and Bhatnagar, O. P., 1998, *Education and Communication for Development*, Oxford and IBH publishing Co. Pvt. Ltd., New Delhi.

MONITORING AND EVALUATION: CONCEPT AND DEFINITION, MONITORING AND EVALUATION OF EXTENSION PROGRAMMES

Definition

1. It is a process of systematically drawing upon experience as a media of making future efforts more effective.
2. Programme evaluation is the determination of the extent to which the desired objectives have been attained or the amount of movement that has been attained or the amount of movement

that has been made in the desired direction.

3. Evaluation is the process of delineating, obtaining and providing useful information for judging decision alternative.

Types of evaluation

1. Self evaluation: This is to be carried out by every worker as a matter of routline. This requires the self critical attitude, which is so essential for extension work.
2. Internal evaluation: Evaluation carried to by the agency responsible for the planning and implementation of the programme. Some of the other methods for internal evaluation are systematic use of diaries and reports of workers, planned visits of staff members to work spots.
3. External evaluation: Evaluation conducted by a person or a committee outside the area of operation.

Purpose of Evaluation

1. **Programme improvement :** Evaluation is the integral part of the education process. It is focused on improvement of this process. We can discover ways and means for improving our educational work.
2. **Programme accomplishments :** Evaluation helps us to determine progress with any activity or job. It also allows us to assess the results of our educational efforts.
3. **Public relation :** Evaluation provide realistic information to report to the public, parliament and legislative bodies.
4. **Profession growth :** Evaluation enhances our knowledge. It gives us an index as to how we are doing as professional workers.
5. **Professional security :** Evaluation provides us with information that gives us satisfaction, a feeling of accomplishment, confidence in ourselves and in the extension education function.
6. **Effective workmanship:** evaluation gives us the opportunity to work together as an extension staff.

7. **Impact of the extension programmes :** Evaluation help to determine the short term and long term impact of the extension programme.
8. **Content of the programme :** Evaluation enables determination of whether the content is contributing to the overall objectives of extension or not.
9. **Method of extension teaching :** Evaluation provides information as to whether the extension teaching methods are being used effectively or not, or whether non extension methods are being used. It also helps in involving new methods of extension.

Thus the purpose of extension evaluation is to discover the extent to which programme objectives are being achieved, to determine the reasons for specific success and failures.

Evaluate Programme Management

1. Appropriate groups and organizations are involved in carrying out the programme.
2. Volunteer local leaders who assisted in carrying out the programme are given adequate training by the extension staff to do the job assigned.
3. To subjected matter presented is current and appropriate to meet the programme objectives.
4. The methods and materials used to present the subject matter are varied and stimulating.
5. Identifies the evidence you need to gather about the criteria work out the methods for collecting the evidence.

Evaluate Programme Results

State the specific objectives to be evaluated in operational terms so they are measurable.

- Collect evidence from the specific group. You are trying to teach.
- Obtain valid and reliable evidence.

- Select appropriate methods for collecting evidence such as observations, personal interviews, mailed questionnaires, group interviews and the like.
- If the total population cannot be included in obtaining evidence, be sure a sample is selected that adequately represents the whole population you are trying to teach.
- Draw only those conclusions about the programme that can logically be derived from the evidence collected.

Contribution to Evaluation

- Contribution help to establish a bench mark. The first principle in programme building i.e. to get the facts about a situation and the first measurement in evaluation must be taken at the point where people start.
- Evaluation shows how far our plans have progressed. Studies of extension work have shown that it after takes years of constant teaching to ensure general adoption of practices.

- Evaluation shows whether we are proceeding in the right direction. It helps to test our objective and recommend changes were needed.
- Evaluation indicates the effectiveness of a programme. After all the end product of our work is to produce educational or material changes. Any good teaching plan must include the process of evaluation.

Evaluation Principles

- Evaluation of a social programme should be in terms of the objectives of the programme.
- Evaluation should include assessment and appraisal of both the product and the process.
- Evaluation should be a continuous process, not just a point in time judgment.

- Evaluation should be made by teams comprising professionals, social scientists and client representatives.
- Evaluation should be done in the context of an organizations philosophy and objectives.
- Evaluation like planning, should takes place at multiple levels.

Extension evaluation process

There are several models of evaluation available in the literature. However, a very simplified version of most of these models may be quite workable for evaluating extension programmes since, as Bhatnagar (1987) has pointed out, any extension evaluation process has to be based on certain assumptions. For example, if some inputs are provided in the form of a programme, specific outputs can be expected and if these outputs happen, then the purpose of the programme can be achieved; if the purpose is achieved, then the development goal is realised. This means that evaluation has to be so designed that the quality types and adequacy of the input measures, outputs and their impact in achieving the programme objectives have to be evaluated systematically. Steps involved in an extension programme evaluative process may be as follows:

- Formulate evaluation objectives Specific objectives to be achieved through the evaluative process must be clearly and adequately identified and started. All further efforts should be knit around these objectives.
- Classify programme objectives It is assumed that each extension programme, when formulated and implemented, will have specific well-defined objectives. Since evaluation is basically a process of determining the extent to which various extension teaching activities were organized and managed and the extent to which they contributed to achieving the goals, programme objectives must be clearly understood and if necessary, further broke down into measurable terms. This is a crucial step as all further efforts will be directed towards collecting evidence related to these objectives.

- Identify indicators To identify indicators or the kind of evidence necessary to evaluate achievement in relation to specified programme objectives, it is necessary that specific beneficiaries of the programme be identified, the kind of behavioural changes expected in them be clearly stated, and the kin of learning experiences expected to be provided to them spelled out, together with the level of management to be achieved for provided those learning experiences are specified. Once this is done, identification of specific indicators to measures the achievements will not be difficult.

- Decide the kind of information needed once the indicators for evaluating the management and performance of a programme have been indicated, specific information to be collected may be worked out. Since there is usually more information than an extension worker can collect, he has to be very discriminating about the kind and amount of information that should be collected. Timing for collection of information may also need to be specified.

- Sampling The purpose of sampling is to take a relatively small number of units from a population in such a way that the evidence collected from them becomes representative evidence of the entire population. Although there are several sampling methods, perhaps stratified sampling procedures may be most suitable for extension evaluation studies a they allow inclusion of all interested groups and ensure enough heterogeneity in the sample.

- Decide the design of evaluation An ideal design of evaluation may be an experimental one. This would allow separating the effect of the programme from other factors, by setting control and treatment groups. Several experimental designs, such as one–group pre–test–post–test design, static groups comparison, pre–test, post–test control group design, Solomon four–group design, longitudinal study design, etc. are available in literature and can be used. However, in actual practice, extension progammes are seldom run in a way that allows an experimental design of evaluation. In Pilot Projects, it might be possible to use an experimental design of evaluation. By and large, a survey method is use. This method can be used for evaluating ongoing progress or as an ex–post facto evaluation of the programme after it has completed its tenure.

- Collection and analysis of evaluation evidence There are many methods for collecting information for evaluative purposes, such as the mail questionnaire, personal interview, distributed questionnaires, group interviews, case studies, systematic field observations, systematic study of secondary data etc. Selection of the right kind of data collection method will depend on the objectives of the evaluation, kind of information needed, time and resources available and the type of respondents from whom information is to be collected.

However, whatever the method used, a specific questionnaire or interview schedule or data recording sheet must be developed with care.

Once the data is collected, it must be tabulated, summarized and analyzed with adequate care. This step should not be rushed. To avoid delay, however, analysis may be done with the help of a computer.

- Interpretation of the results in a proper way It is a very crucial as evaluation results can be missed also. Once tentative generalizations are arrived at, it may be appropriate and they are informally discussed among the interpreters as well as with programme planning and implementation officials, so that the results of evaluation are put in a proper perspective.

The evaluation results must clearly state the achievements, failures and future adjustments needed. A written report of the evaluation findings should be prepared and made available to all concerned.

References

1. De, D. and Jirli, B. (2010). A Handbook of Extension Education. Agrobios (India), Jodhpur.
2. Mondal, S. (2019). Fundamentals of Agricultural Extension Education. Kalyani publishers, New Delhi.
3. Adivi Reddy, A., 2001, *Extension Education*, Sree Lakshmi press, Bapatla.
4. Dahama, O. P. and Bhatnagar, O. P., 1998, *Education and Communication for Development*, Oxford and IBH publishing Co. Pvt. Ltd., New Delhi.
5. Jalihal, K. A. and Veerabhadraiah, V., 2007, *Fundamentals of Extension Education and Management in Extension*, Concept publishing company, New Delhi.

CHAPTER THIRTEEN

CAPACITY BUILDING OF EXTENSION PERSONNEL AND FARMERS

Capacity Building can be defined as "activities which strengthen the knowledge, abilities, skills and behavior of individuals and improve institutional structures and processes such that the organization can efficiently meet its mission and goals in a sustainable way. Training is one of the essential components of capacity building.

Training for Development

Training has become an inseparable part of HRD. It has become one of the components, which enables any institution to churn out its employees as the most productive and most suitable ones.

Training – Definitions

1. Training is the art of increasing the knowledge and skill of an employee for doing a particular job.
2. Training is a learning process, which seeks a relatively permanent change in behavior that occurs as a result of

experience.

3. Training is the process of aiding employees to gain effectiveness in their present or future work through the development of appropriate habits of thought, action, skills, knowledge and attitude **(Milton Mall, 1980)**.

4. Training is the process of changing employee behaviour, attitudes, or opinion through some type of guided experience **(Krietner, 1989)**.

5. Training is a systematic process of changing the behavior, knowledge and or motivation of present employees to improve the match between employee characteristic and employment requirement **(Milkovich and Boudreau, 1998)**

Need for training

The process of training has caught up mainly in industries. This can be attributed to the sudden and competitive change that is occurring in the world. However, the needs for training can be fixed down to the following:

- Rapid changes in technologies and jobs people do.
- Immediate and long term skill shortage
- Changes in the expectation and composition of work force
- Competition and market pressure for improvement in quality of products and services.

Types of training given to extension personnel – This is of broadly two types

1. **Pre-service Training** It is a process through which the individuals are made ready to enter a certain kind professional job, as in agriculture, medicine or engineering. It is a professional training prior to any appointment, oriented to make an individual prepared to enter into a new profession. Swanson (1984) defines it as a programme of training activities that prepares an individual for a career in extension, and usually

leads to some type of diploma, certificate, degree, or other qualification in one or more of the following agriculture, fisheries, forestry, animal and/or veterinary science or home science.

The state departments of Agriculture now prefer University graduates for entry into their extension services and similarly the Veterinary department prefers to to take only Veterinary graduates released from the Universities.

1. **In-Service Training** It is meant for in service candidates who are on the job. In-service training is a process of staff development for the purpose of improving the performance of an incumbent holding a position with assigned job responsibilities. It promotes the professional growth of individuals. In-service training is a problem centred, learner oriented and

time-bound series of activities, which provide the opportunity to develop a sense of purpose. broaden perception of the participants and increase their capacity to gain knowledge and mastery of techniques.

According to Arnon (1987), even for the University graduate, learning cannot cease on completion of formal studies. He said that the in-service training is given with the following objectives

1. To keep up with research by regular meetings between researchers and extension workers, joint colloquia etc.
2. To impart basic knowledge not only in the fields directly related to agriculture, but also in sociology, economics, psychology etc.
3. To improve extension methods, by constant evaluation of methods, the joint study of research findings and extension methods, exchange of experiences. In-Service training are of different types, some of them are as follows:

1. Orientation Training

This training is given usually to newly appointed extension personnel. It provides an introduction to public employment and provides answers to questions which a newly recruited person is likely to ask. This term is also used for training in-service extension personnel in a new responsibility likes a new operational programme so that personnel are appropriately oriented towards meeting the requirements of new situation.

2. Induction / portal / vestibule Training

Induction training is given to new extension personnel immediately after they have been employed and before they are assigned to work in particular area usually as an Assistant Agriculture Officer or Agriculture Officer, or Extension Officer.

3. Maintenance or refresher training

This training is originally started for trainers of the training institutes and Universities for refreshing their knowledge and skills for imparting them to trainees. The term indicates any new training for updating professional competence of extension personnel notably in the subject matter area of specialization. This training is usually imparted in the later career of extension personnel. This training is having considerable importance to extension personnel as it relates to updating to technical knowledge and competence of extension personnel. This deals with new information and new methods and review of older materials. This type of training is given to the employees to keep them at their peak performance level and also prevent them from getting into a rut.

4. Retraining

It refers to the efforts designed to prepare an individual for a new assignment or a broadened aspect of the old specialty.

5. **Career or development training / Training for professional qualification**

This type of training is designed to upgrade the knowledge, skills and ability of employees to help them assume greater responsibility in higher positions. This training may lead to the acquisition of higher degree (undergraduate or postgraduate) or diploma by the employees, to motivate them to move up higher levels of administrative hierarchy (promotions) The Directorate of Extension is operating such a scheme on an yearly basis under which, in addition to salary and allowances which personnel get from their own employing organizations, it pays fixed monthly stipends to extension personnel to cover their cost of boarding, lodging and tuition fees. Only meritorious extension personnel and that too below the age of 45 years are eligible for such courses.

References

1. De, D. and Jirli, B. (2010). A Handbook of Extension Education. Agrobios (India), Jodhpur.
2. Mondal, S. (2019). Fundamentals of Agricultural Extension Education. Kalyani publishers, New Delhi.
3. Adivi Reddy, A., 2001, *Extension Education*, Sree Lakshmi press, Bapatla.
4. Dahama, O. P. and Bhatnagar, O. P., 1998, *Education and Communication for Development*, Oxford and IBH publishing Co. Pvt. Ltd., New Delhi.
5. Jalihal, K. A. and Veerabhadraiah, V., 2007, *Fundamentals of Extension Education and Management in Extension*, Concept publishing company, New Delhi.
6. Muthaiah Manoraharan, P. and Arunachalam, R., *Agricultural Extension*, Himalaya Publishing House (Mumbai).

7. Rathore, O. S. *et al.*, 2012, *Handbook of Extension Education,* Agrotech Publishing Academy, Udaipur.

CHAPTER FOURTEEN

COMMUNICATION

According to Leagans (1961), Communication is the process by which two or more people exchange ideas, facts, feelings or impressions in ways that each gains a common understanding of the meaning, intent and use of messages. The term 'communication' stems from the Latin word 'communis'-meaning' 'common'. Communication, then, is a conscious attempt to share information, ideas, attitudes and the like with others. In essence it is the act of getting a sender and a receiver tuned together for a particular message, or a series of message. "Communication means the movement of knowledge to people in such ways that they act on that knowledge to achieve some useful result. This result may range all the way from a small improvement in doing some productive task, to the generation of a sense of national unity and strength in a country. Communication in this sense includes the whole learning process. It encompasses the teacher- the message or material to be taught- the means or media used to carry the message -the treatment given by those media- the learning achieved by the audience or student- and the actions by which the learning is put into practice". (Winfield (1957).

According to Leagans (1961), Communication is the process by which two or more people exchange ideas, facts, feelings or impressions in ways that each gains a common understanding of the meaning, intent and use of messages. The term 'communication' stems from the Latin word 'communis'-meaning' 'common'.

Communication, then, is a conscious attempt to share information, ideas, attitudes and the like with others. In essence it is the act of getting a sender and a receiver tuned together for a particular message, or a series of message. "Communication means the movement of knowledge to people in such ways that they act on that knowledge to achieve some useful result. This result may range all the way from a small improvement in doing some productive task, to the generation of a sense of national unity and strength in a country. Communication in this sense includes the whole learning process. It encompasses the teacher- the message or material to be taught- the means or media used to carry the message -the treatment given by those media- the learning achieved by the audience or student- and the actions by which the learning is put into practice". (Winfield (1957).

Importance of Communication

1. Communication establishes a favourable climate in which development can take place.
2. Communication has multiplier effect
3. Communication varies the aspirations of the people
4. Communication is essential for all human activities
5. Communication is essential for good leadership

Elements of Communication

The Communicator

This is the person who starts the process of communication in operation. He is the source or originator of messages. He is the sender of messages. He is the first to give expression to message intended to reach an audience in a manner that results in correct interpretation and desirable response. When a communicator does not hold the confidence of his audience, communication as conceived will not take place.

The following are **the good qualities of a good communicator**

1. The Communicator Knows -

   a. the specifically defined objectives.
   b. the needs, interests, abilities etc. of the audience.
   c. the content, validity, usefulness and importance of the message
   d. the channels that will reach the audience and their usefulness
   e. the tactics of organising and treating the message
   f. his/her professional abilities and limitations.

2. The communicator is interested in -

   a. the intended audience and their welfare
   b. the specific message and its effects in helping the people
   c. the entirety of communication process
   d. the proper use and limitation of communication channels.

3. The communicator prepares -

   a. a specific teaching plan for communication
   b. materials and equipments needed for communication
   c. a plan for evaluation of results.

4. The communicator has skill in

   a. selecting messages
   b. treating messages
   c. expressing messages in verbal and written forms
   d. the selection and use of channels
   e. understanding the audience
   f. collecting evidence of results.

In contrast to the above, the following are **the qualities of a poor communicator**

- Fail to have ideas to present that are really useful to the audience.

- Fail to give the complete story and show its relationship to people's problems
- Forget that time and energy are needed to absorb the material presented.
- Feel they are always clearly understood.
- Refuse to adjust to 'closed' minds.
- Talk while others are not listening.
- Get far too ahead of audience understanding.
- Fail to recognise others' view - point and develop presentation accordingly
- Fail to recognise that communication is a two-way process.
- Let their own biases over-influence the presentation.
- Fail to see that everyone understands questions brought up for discussion
- Fail to provide a permissive atmosphere.
- Disregard the values, customs, prejudices and habits of people with whom they attempt to communicate.
- Fail to start where people are, with respect to knowledge, skill, interest and need.

Message or content

A message is the information communicator wishes his audience to receive, understand, accept and act upon. Messages, for example, may consist of statements of scientific facts about agriculture, sanitation or nutrition; description of action being taken by individuals, groups or committees; reasons why certain kinds of action should be taken ; or steps necessary in taking given kinds of action.

Features of a good message A good message must be -

- In line with the objectives to be attained.
- Clearly understandable by the audience
- In line with the mental, social, economic and physical capabilities of the audience

- Significant-economically, socially or aesthetically to the needs, interests and values of the audience.
- Specific in terms of audience and locale
- Accurate so as to be scientifically sound, factual and current in nature.
- Appropriate to the channel selected.
- Appealing and attractive to the audience signifying the utility values and immediacy of use.
- Adequate in such a way to have effective proportionate combination of principle and practice manageable so as to be handled by the communicator within the resources availability.

In contrast, poor communicators often commit the following which mar the effectiveness of message sending

1. Fail to clearly separate the key message from the supporting content or subject-matter.
2. Fail to prepare and organise their message properly.
3. Use inaccurate of 'fuzzy' symbols-words, visuals, or real objects- to represent the message.
4. Fail to select messages that are sharply in line with the felt needs of the audience.
5. Fail to present the message objectively-present the material, often biased, to support only one side of the proposition.
6. Fail to view the message from the standpoint of the audience.
7. Fail to time the message properly within a presentation or within a total programme.

Selecting and 'packaging' messages so they have a good chance of being understood, accepted and acted upon when received is a crucial step in the communication process. It is one of the six keys to success in efforts to influence people to change their ways of thinking and of doing that lead to social and economic improvement.

Channels of Communication

The sender and the receiver of messages must be connected or 'tuned' with each other. For this purpose, channels of communication are necessary. They are the physical bridges between the sender and the receiver of messages-the avenues between a communicator and an audience on which messages travel to and fro. They are the transmission lines used for carrying messages to their destination. Thus, the channels serve as essential tools of the communicator.

A channel may be anything used by a sender of messages to connect him with intended receivers. The crucial point is that he must get in contact with his audience. The message must get through.

However, channels are no good without careful direction or use in the right way, at the right time, to do the right job, for the right purpose with the right audience, all in relation to the right message. So, proper selection and use of channels constitutes a third determinant of successful communication. Without proper use of channels, messages, no matter how important, will not get through to the intended audience.

Many obstructions can enter channels. These are often referred to as **'noise'** - that is, some obstruction that prevents the message from being heard by or carried over clearly to the audience. 'Noise' emerges from a wide range of sources and causes.

Sources and causes for noise:

1. *Failure of a channel to reach the intended audience.* Usually, no one channel will reach an entire audience. Some examples: Meetings-all people cannot or may not attend. Radio-all people do not have access to a receiving set or may not be tuned in if they did. **Written** *material*-many people cannot read, and others may not.

2. *Failure on the part of a communicator to handle channels skillfully.* If a meeting, tour, radio programme or any other

channel is not used according to good procedure and technique, its potential for carrying a message is dissipated.

3. *Failure to select channels appropriates to the objective of a communicator.* All channels are not equally useful in attaining a specific objective.

4. **Failure to use channels in accordance with the abilities of the audience.** Written materials, for example, cannot serve as useful channels for communicating information to people who are unable to read or to understand the level of complexity or abstraction of the message.

5. **Failure to avoid physical distraction.** When using the channel of meetings, for example, distractions including people moving in and out, loud noises in or out of the group, heat, lighting, crowded condition and many other forms of distraction often obstruct successful message sending.

6. **Failure of an audience to listen or look carefully.** The only messages that get through to an audience are those which are heard, seen or experienced. An unfortunate tendency of people is not to give undivided attention to the communicator. This is a powerful obstruction that prevents messages from reaching desired destination.

7. **Failure to use enough channels in parallel.** The more channels a communicator uses in parallel or at about the same time,. the more chances he has for the message getting through and being properly received . No single channel will ordinarily reach all people who need to receive a message. Research indicates that up to five or six channels used in combination are often necessary to get a message through to large numbers of people with enough impact to influence significant changes in behaviour.

8. ***Use of too many channels in a series.*** An important principle of communication is that the more channels used in a series the less chance a communicator has for getting his message through to the intended audience. In this context, the following principles are to be borne in mind : (1) The more steps by which the communicator is removed from his intended receiver, the greater are his chances of losing the proper message. (2) When lines of communication get too long for assured communication they can be improved in two primary ways : (a) by using additional channels in parallel, and (b) by eliminating some of the channels in the series.

Treatment of Messages

Treatment has to do with the way a message is handled to get the information across to an audience. It relates to the technique, or details of procedure, or manner of performance, essential to expertness in presenting messages. Hence, treatment deals with the design of methods for presenting messages. Designing the methods for treating messages does not relate to formulation of the message or to the selection of channels, but to the technique employed for presentation within the situation provided by a message and a channel.

The purpose of treatment is to make the message clear, understandable and realistic to the audience. Designing treatment usually requires original thinking, deep insight into the principles of human behaviour and skill in creating and using refined techniques of message presentation.

Treatment of messages can be varied in an almost infinite number of ways. The following are the three categories of bases useful for varying treatment

A. Matters of general organisation

1. Repetition of frequency of mention of ideas and concepts. Contrast of ideas.

2. Chronological-compared to logical, compared to psychological.
3. Presenting one side compared to two sides of an issue.

4. Emotional compared to logical appeals.
5. Starting with strong arguments compared to saving them until the end of presentation.
6. Inductive compared to deductive.
7. Proceeding from the general to the specific and *vice versa*.
8. Explicitly drawing conclusions compared to leaving conclusions implicit for the audience to draw.

C. Matters of speaking and acting

1. Limit the scope of presentation to a few basic ideas and to the time allotted. Too many ideas at one time are confusing.
2. Be yourself. You can't be anyone else. Strive to be clear, not clever.
3. Know the facts. Fuzziness means sure death to a message.
4. Don't read your speech. People have more respect for a communicator who is sure of his subject.
5. Know the audience. Each audience has its own personality. Be responsive to it.
6. Avoid being condescending. Do not talk or act *down* to people, or over their heads.
7. Decide on the dramatic effect desired. In addition to the content of messages, a communicator should be concerned with 'showmanship'. Effective treatment requires sincerity, smoothness, enthusiasm, warmth, flexibility and appropriateness of voice, gestures, movements and tempo.
8. Use alternative communicators when appropriate, as in group discussions, panels, interviews, etc. Remember that audience appeal is a psychological bridge to getting a message delivered.

9. Quit on time. Communicators who stop when they are 'finished' are rewarded by audience goodwill.

D. Matters of symbol variation and devices for representing ideas

To represent ideas by effective treatment with reference to the desired behavioural changes, a variety of audio-visual aids may be used. Communicators should be aware that teaching message to achieve maximum audience impact is a highly professional task. Treatment is a creative task that has to be 'tailor-made' for each instance of communication. Experience, thinking and planning, skill in verbalisation and writing, understanding of the principles of teaching and learning, knowledge of a) the subject b) the audience to be reached and c) skill in the use of channels etc will help the communicator to undertake the process of message treatment.

The Audience

An audience is the intended receiver of message. It is the consumer of messages. It is the intended respondent in message sending, and is assumed to be in a position to gain economically, socially or in other ways by responding to the message in particular ways. In good communication the communicator already identifies the audience aims.

The importance of clearly identifying an audience cannot be over-stressed. The more homogeneous an audience, the greater the chances of successful communication. Likewise, the more a communicator knows about his audience and can pin-point its characteristics the more likely he is to make an impact.

The following are some of the issues to clarify the nature of audience:

1. Communication channels established by the social organisation.
2. The system of values held by the audience-what they think is important.
3. Forces influencing group conformity-custom, tradition etc.

4. Individual personality factors-susceptibility to change etc.
5. Native and acquired abilities.
6. Educational, economic and social levels.
7. Pressure of occupational responsibility-how busy or concerned they are.
8. People's needs as they see them, and as the professional communicator sees them.
9. Why the audience is in need of changed ways of thinking, feeling and doing.
10. How the audience views the situation.

It is useful to a communicator to understand these and other traits of an audience in making his plan for communication.

Audience Response

This is the terminating element in communication applied to rural development programmes. Response by an audience to messages received is in the form of some kind of action of some degree, mentally or physically. Action, therefore, should be viewed as a product, not as a process; it should be dealt with as an end, not as a means. Consequently, the five elements hither to analysed *viz.,* communicator, message, channel, treatment and audience are intended to be viewed as an organised scheme (means) for attaining the desired action (end) on the part of an intended audience.

The number of possible kinds and degrees of response to messages received are almost infinite. The following gives an idea of possible variety in response that may result when a useful message is received by the intended audience:

1. **Understanding Vs knowledge**. Knowledge of facts alone does not constitute understanding. It is only the first step. Understanding is attained only when one is able to attach meaning to facts, see the relationship of facts to each other and to the whole of a proposition and the relationship of the total body of facts to the problem under consideration. Communicative efforts often fails because it stops simply

with laying facts before people and does not continue in a systematic way to promote an understanding of the facts presented. People usually do not act on facts alone, but only when an understanding of facts is gained. Communication must promote understanding.

2. **Acceptance Vs rejection**. A free, alert and thinking human mind requires that understanding precede acceptance of facts and propositions. In turn, it insists on mental acceptance before resorting to action. For it is what human beings come to believe, not what they merely know or even understand, that determines what they do when they are free to act as they choose

3. **Remembering vs. forgetting**. When opportunity for action is not immediately available or action is delayed, the factor of forgetting what was learned influences the kind and extent of action taken at any point of time in the future. This basic principle has extensive implications for timing in communication programmes. Transmitting the right message to the right people at the right time is often a crucial factor in successful communication.

4. **Mental Vs physical action.** Changes in the mind of man, must always precede changes in the actions of his hands. In short, man's mind controls his overt behaviour. Consequently, a message suggesting physical action could receive all the mental action required, except the final decision to act. This is sometimes referred to as 'lip service'.

5. **Right vs. wrong**. The intent of a communication is to promote desirable action by an audience as determined by the communicator and expressed in his objectives. Consequently, resulting action in line with the intended objectives is assumed to be 'right' action. But the problem is more complex. Unfortunately, 'noise' often plays mischief at this point. For a variety of reasons, people often fail to behave precisely according to instructions, even when they

understand and accept them.

References

1. De, D. and Jirli, B. (2010). A Handbook of Extension Education. Agrobios (India), Jodhpur.
2. Mondal, S. (2019). Fundamentals of Agricultural Extension Education. Kalyani publishers, New Delhi.
3. Adivi Reddy, A., 2001, *Extension Education*, Sree Lakshmi press, Bapatla.
4. Dahama, O. P. and Bhatnagar, O. P., 1998, *Education and Communication for Development*, Oxford and IBH publishing Co. Pvt. Ltd., New Delhi.
5. Jalihal, K. A. and Veerabhadraiah, V., 2007, *Fundamentals of Extension Education and Management in Extension*, Concept publishing company, New Delhi.
6. Muthaiah Manoraharan, P. and Arunachalam, R., *Agricultural Extension*, Himalaya Publishing House (Mumbai).
7. Rathore, O. S. *et al.*, 2012, *Handbook of Extension Education*, Agrotech Publishing Academy, Udaipur.

CHAPTER FIFTEEN

COMMUNICATION MODELS

Models- Definitions

In social science research, a model is a tentative description of what a social process, say the communication process or a system might be like. It is a tool of explanation and analyses, very often in a diagrammatic form, to show how the various elements of a situation being studied relate to each other. Models are not statements of reality. Only after much further research and testing would the model is considered viable. It could then be developed into a theory. The term model can also refer to a particular process or object, which is used as a point of reference, when an attempt to explain the unknown is being made. It comprises involving an analogy to throw up the similarities between the phenomena to be explained and one, which is well known, i.e. the model.

Additionally the model can be a person whose behaviour others wish to emulate or who they wish to model themselves after.

The simplest definition of a model is that it is an analogue. A model is a relatively well- developed analogy. Given two objects or processes, which are dissimilar in many respects, one is an analogue of the other to the extent that the physical or logical structure of one re-presents the physical or logical structure of the other.

The advantage of models in communication research is that it allows the researcher to account for different variables in different communication situations. Models only represent systems or processes. Since they are not real, they are just symbolic ways of looking at systems to help us to think about them more lucidly. Again since models do not show every part of a system, they are usually incomplete in that sense. Even those that arc shown are represented only in enough detail to help us look at the processes or features in which we are interested. Mo0dels give us an idea of complicated objects or events in a general way. They enable us to see how a particular communication event fits into the general pattern. They provide a classification for an orderly nature of events and suggest new ways of looking at old problems, and familiar events. They help us by providing a structure of reference for purposes of study. Theories are not models and the most fundamental difference between a theory and a model is that the former is an explanation whereas the latter is a representation.

Communication Models

Aristotle's Model of Communication

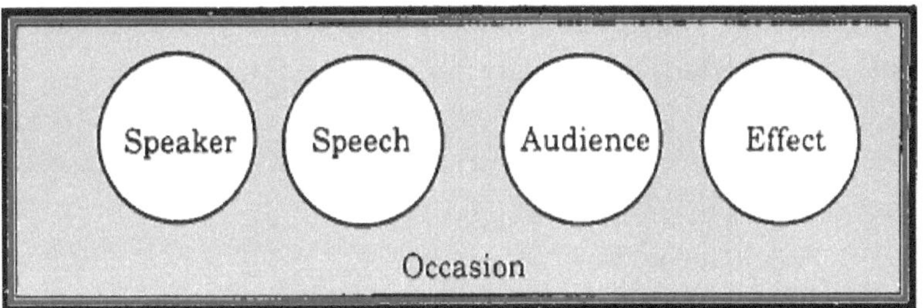

Aristotle's Model of Communication (Devito, 1978)

The earliest model of communication was the symmetrical and simple model developed by the great Greek philosopher Aristotle some 2000 years before. Aristotle in his model includes the five essential elements of communication, i.e., the speaker, the speech or message, the audience, the occasion, and the effect. In his rhetoric, Aristotle advises the speaker on constructing a speech for different audiences on different occasions for different effects. This model is most applicable to public speaking.

Lasswell's Model (1948)

Lasswell has given us another simple model. His model belongs specifically to the area of mass communication. He argued that to understand the process of mass communication one needs to study each of the stages in his mode. "Who says what, in which channel, to whom, and, with what effect."

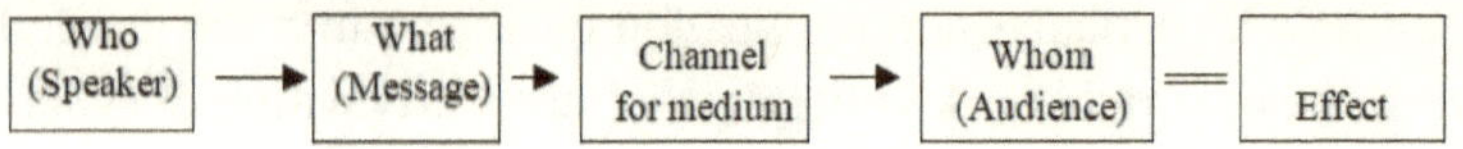

(Source: Public Opinion and Propaganda by Harold Lasswell, 1948)

This is the verbal version of Shannon and Weaver's original model. It is linear. It sees communication as the transmission of message. It raises the issue of the effect rather than meaning. Effect implies an observable and measurable change in the receiver that is caused by identifiable elements in the process. A change in one of these elements will change the effect. We can change the encoder. We can change the message. We can change the channel, and each one of these changes would produce the appropriate change in the effect. Most mass communication research has implicitly followed this model.

The work of institutions and their process on the producers of communication on the audience and how it is affected clearly derives from a process based linear model.

Lasswell's model - comments

Until the 1960s Lasswell's four questions (of who says what, by what channel, to whom and with what effect) dominated studies of the mass media in France. Not only his exemplary expression defines the different research areas for communication investigations, but also seemed to prescribe the appropriate concepts and methodological orientation to be followed. Thus,

Lasswell's paradigm served the entire scientific community of communication scholars.

This Lasswell model was represented by Michael Buhler.

<table>
<tr><td rowspan="2">Situation
depending on the
human sciences</td><td>WHO</td><td></td><td>TO WHOM</td></tr>
<tr><td>Transmitter</td><td></td><td>Receiver</td></tr>
<tr><td></td><td colspan="3">BY WHAT CHANNEL</td></tr>
<tr><td rowspan="2">Situation nearing
the physical
sciences</td><td>SAYS WHAT</td><td colspan="2">WITH WHAT EFFECTS</td></tr>
<tr><td>Message Stimulus</td><td colspan="2">Influence reply</td></tr>
</table>

Lasswell's Communication Model

It was Harold Lasswell who first precisely delineated the various elements, which constitute a "communication fact." According to him, one cannot suitably describe a "communication action" without answering the following questions: who said what, by what channel, to whom and with what effect?

Identification of transmitters, analysis of message content, study of transmission channels audience identification and evaluation of effects; these are the five parameters of communication studies. Michel Buhler represents the Lasswell model with the above diagram.

Along with other developments during this period were a number of writings that sought to provide description of the nature of the communication process. One of the most often cited political scientists Harold Lasswell advanced characterization communication in 1948 as an outgrowth of his work in the area of propaganda. Lasswell provided a general view of communication that extended well beyond the boundaries of political science. Lasswell's view of communication, as had Aristotle has some two thousand years earlier, focused primarily on verbal messages. It also emphasized the elements of speaker, messages, and audience, but used different terms. Both men viewed communication as a one way process in which one individual influenced others through messages. Lasswell offered a broadened of definition channel to include mass media along with verbal speech as a part of the communication process. His approach also provided a more generalized view of the goal or effect of communication than did the Aristotelian perspective. Lasswell's work suggested that there could be a variety of outcomes or effects of communication such as to inform, to entertain, to aggravate and to persuade (Brent, 1984).

Shannon and Weaver Model (1949)

The preconceptions of the academic field of mass communication were heavily influenced by the engineering model of Shannon and Weaver (1949) Communication was conceived as a linear act of transmission of a message from a source to a receiver via a signal producing transmitter. A component called 'noise' acknowledged the presence of context in the electrical engineering model.

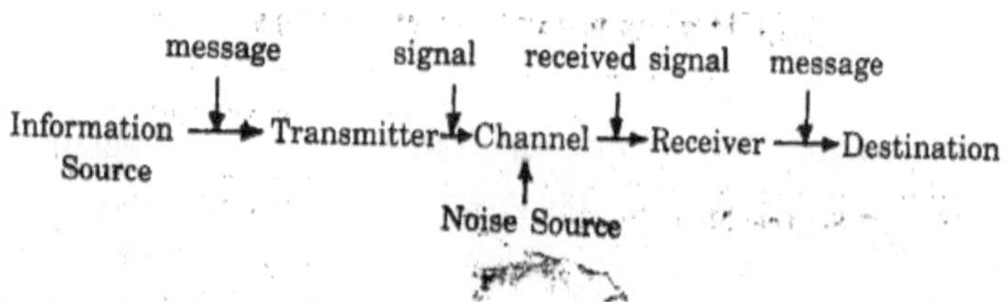

Source: The Mathematical Theory of Communication, Claude E. Shannon and Warren Weaver, 1949

Shannon and Weaver Model

Shannon and Weaver's mathematical theory of communication (1949) is widely accepted as one of the main seeds out of which communication studies have grown. It is a clear example of the process school, seeing communication as the transmissions of messages. The work developed during the Second World War in the Bell telephone laboratories in the US and their main concern was to work out ways in which channels of communication could be used most efficiently. For them, the main channels were the telephone, cable and the radio wave. They produced a theory that enabled them to approach the problem of how to send a maximum amount of information along a given channel to carry information. This concentration on the channel and its capacity is appropriate to their engineering and mathematical background, but they claim that their theory is widely applicable over the whole question of human communication.

Shannon and Weaver's model (1949) presents communication as a linear process. Its simplicity has attracted many derivatives, and its linear process centered nature has attracted many critics. It's obvious characteristics of simplicity and linearity standout clearly.

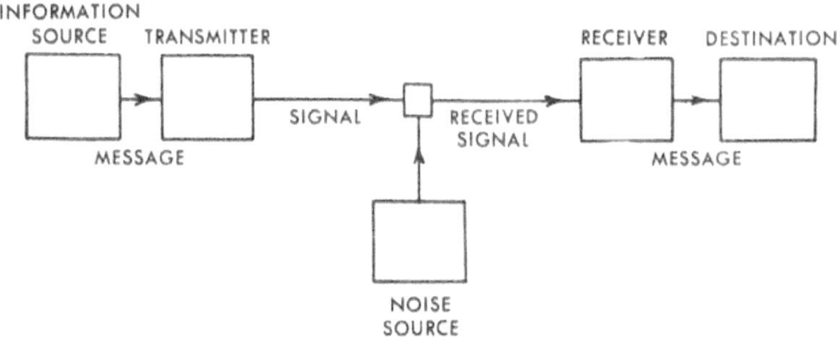

(Source: The Mathematical theory of communication. Claude E. *Shannon* and Warren Weaver, 1949)

Claude Shannon and Warren Weaver gave this model. As the diagram above indicates, this communication model comprises four elements. A source of information, with a greater or lesser number of messages to communicate; a transmitter or sender with the capacity to transform a message into a signal; a receiver which decodes the signal in order to retrieve the initial message, and finally, the destination, a person or thing for whom the message is intended. Communication, according to this model, follows a simple left to right process. The information source (say speaker), selects a desired message from all the possible messages. The message is sent through a transmitter (microphone) and is changed into signals. A receiver (say earphone), changed back into a message and given to the destination, a listener, receives the signals. In the process of transmission, certain distortions are added to the signal which are not part of the message and these will be called noise.

The basis of all contemporary Western theories of Communication - Shannon- Weaver model stresses the idea of inside and outside and assumes that communication is a lineal matching rather than making. The information source changes the message into the signal, which is actually sent over the communication channel from the transmitter to the receiver. In the case of telephony the channel is a wire the signal a varying electrical current on this wire, the transmitter is the set of devices (telephone transmitter etc.) which change the sound pressure of the voice into the varying electric current. In oral speech, the information source is the brain, the transmitter is the voice mechanism producing the varying sound pressure (the signal) which is transmitted through the air (the channel). In radio, the channel is simply space, and the signal is the electromagnetic wave, which is transmitted. The receiver is an inverse transmitter, changing the transmitted signal back into a message and handing this message on to the destination.

In the process of being transmitted, usually certain things are added to the signal, which were not intended by the sender. These additions are distortion of sounds as in telephony, or static in radios, or errors in transmission in telegraphy or facsimile etc., Such changes in transmission signals are called noise.

Shannon and Weaver's Model (1949) comments

Both European and American scholars recognize that Shannon and Weaver's (1949) model provided the basic paradigm for effects-oriented communication research by setting forth the main elements (source, channel, messages, receiver) of a simple linear model of communication. This model became tremendously popular with communication researchers enabling the field of communication study to take off' about 30 years ago. It formed the main paradigm around which invisible college of communication researcher formed. Less well known is the contribution by Shannon and Weaver in defining the concept of information as a central notion for the field of Communication. Shannon and Weaver's model was used in the field of electronics for many purposes, form the design of telephone networks to matrices of computer memories. An eminent Finnish scholar between the two central concept (a) communication (b) informations has identified an important distinction. These two concepts trace from Aristotle to the Shannon and Weaver mathematical theory of a single transmission and to other models of information and communication. Although Shannon and Weaver's concept of the probabilistic model of communication has been fruitful in leading to further research, it was never intended to describe linguistic information and human communication. (Source: Everett Rogers and Francis Balle, 1985).

C.E. Osgood - Schramm Model (1975)

To the circular model, we have added boxes and arrows showing the influence of noise and personality are a helix used as a model by Frank E.X. Dance. He felt that circular models were better than straight - lines ones like Shannon- Weaver, but that they had a built in error since they showed communication ending up where it started off. In fact as an act of communication goes on, the noise gets less (because the communicators get more used to handling the channel / model) and personality becomes more helpful (because, as communicators get to know each other and the subject, they adjust to each other and fill gaps in their knowledge).

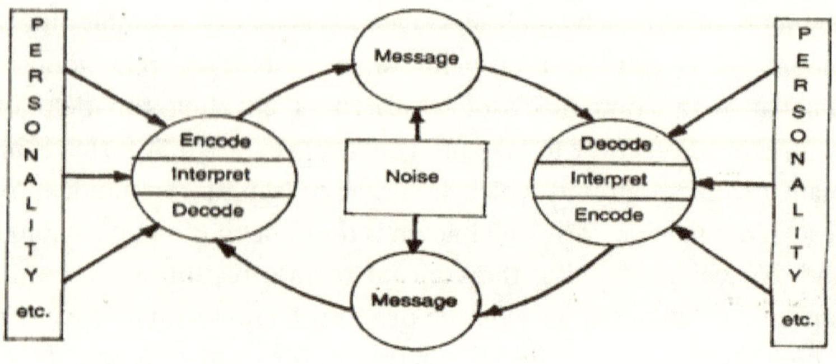

C.E. Osgood-Schramm Communication modelEnter Caption

David Berlo's Model (1960)

In the last twenty-five years, a number of models of communication have been developed by communicologists, each one expanding the earlier presentation. David Berlo's model is one among them, which has been profusely quoted and frequently mentioned in discussions. In his book, "The Process of Communication" written in 1960, he presented this model which has a close similarity to the earlier Aristotelian model, including the traditional elements of source, message, channel and receiver. Berlo's model attempts to explain the various components in the communication process. For each of these basic components, controlling factors were listed.

For each of these four components there are five elements that need to be considered. The source and receiver are treated in essentially the same way. To study either we need to consider their communication skills (speaking and writing for the source and listening and reading for the receiver) their attitudes, their knowledge, the social system of which they are a part and the culture in which they operate. The message consists of both elements and structure, each of which may be broken down into content, treatment and code. For the channel, Berlo lists the five senses, emphasizing that the messages may be sent and received by any and all of the senses.

Berlo more than the others emphasized the idea that communication was a process, and the idea that "meanings are in people, not in words...."

109

CHAPTER SIXTEEN

ADOPTION AND DIFFUSION OF INNOVATIONS

Diffusion and adoption are closely interrelated even though they are conceptually distinct. Diffusion of Innovations is a theory that seeks to explain how, why, and at what rate new ideas and technology spread through cultures.

Diffusion of Innovations is a theory that seeks to explain how, why, and at what rate new ideas and technology spread through cultures. Everett Rogers, a professor of rural sociology, popularized the theory in his 1962 book Diffusion of Innovations. He said diffusion is the process by which an innovation is communicated through certain channels over time among the members of a social system. The origins of the diffusion of innovations theory are varied and span multiple disciplines.

Diffusion of innovations refers to the spread of those innovations through a population, and is simply the result of a host of individual adoption decisions. According to Rogers 1962 the diffusion process can be explained as "the spread of a new idea from its source of invention or creation to its ultimate use of adopters". The process by which an innovation spreads within a social system is called "***diffusion***". An innovation diffuses within a social system through its "*adoption*" by individual and groups.

Diffusion and its Components

Definition

Diffusion is the process by which an innovation is communicated through certain channels over time among the members of a social system. Meaning It is a special and significant type of communication in that the messages are dealing only the novel ideas generated in the laboratory to be spread among a larger number of social systems. It is the newness of the idea in the message content of communication that adds diffusion its special trait and importance.

Elements of Diffusion

- Innovation
- Channels
- Overtime
- Members of the social system

Innovation: It is an idea which is a new one supposed to be adopted by the intended clientele. It may not always hold objectivity due to lapse of time since its discovery.

Channel: It is the mean or transmission lines through which the innovation is communicated to reach its audience.

Overtime: It is the time period in which an innovation takes its own pace to spread. It may be faster or moderate or slower based on the innovation's importance.

Members of the social system: It is the degree to which an innovation reaches a significant group of individuals to accept and adopt the new idea being implemented. High cost farm equipment may be difficult to be tried in small parts.

An innovation is an idea, practice or object that is perceived as new by an individual or other unit of adoption. Perception is an activity through which an individual becomes aware of objects around oneself and of events taking place. The technologies, practices developed through research are innovations. These may be new varieties of crops and plants, new breeds of livestock, new chemicals and medicines, new technique of doing things etc. Farmers themselves may develop some new practices which are also innovations. Irrespective of the time period the idea or practice was originally developed, when a person first becomes aware of it, it is an innovation to that person.

Perceived attributes of Innovations

Attributes are qualities, characteristics or traits possessed by an object. An innovation has some qualities or characteristics. It is not the intrinsic quality, but the quality or character of the innovation as people see to them, is important for extension. The perceived attributes of innovations which are which are basic to extension are as follows.

Relative Advantage: The degree to which an innovation is perceived as better than the idea it supersedes. The relative advantage may have a number of dimensions. For example, if a new technology or practice gives more yield or income; or saves time, labour and cost; or has less risk than the existing one; it has more relative advantage, multiple use of an innovation may be a form of relative advantage. For example, an equipment or material which may be used for a number of activities has more advantage than an equipment or material which can be used for a single purpose. The advantage of location for specific enterprises in specific areas may provide some relative advantage. The innovations which have more relative advantage are likely to be adopted quickly.

Compatibility: The degree to which an innovation is perceived as being consistent with the existing values, past experiences and needs of the potential adopters. Compatibility has at least two dimensions situational compatibility and cultural compatibility. When a new crop variety suits the agro- climate condition of the farmer, it indicates situational compatibility. When a breed of live-stick advocated to the farmers is in agreement with their beliefs and values, it is cultural compatibility. The name given to an innovation may affect its compatibility. Compatibility of an innovation is essential for its adoption.

Complexity: The degree to which an innovation is perceived as difficult to understand and use. An innovation should, as far as possible, be less complex for the farmers to understand and use. However, complexity of an innovation may not deter its adoption, provided it has more relative advantage. For example, many of the high yielding technologies like HYV crops, crossbred cattle, composite fish-culture etc. are quite complex. Still, their diffusion has been quite high, which may be due to their high relative advantage in terms of more yield and income and shorter gestation period.

Complex technologies often require complementary adoption. For example, adoption of high yielding technologies requires adoption of balanced nutrition practices, appropriate protection technology and better management methods, to get the best results. Complex technologies, because of their complicated and intricate nature, require consistent trainings and communication support for the clientele, for their adoption and continued use.

Trialability: The degree to which an innovation may be experimented on a limited basis. Adoption of new seeds and fertilizers are more, compared to new farm machinery, simply because seeds and fertilizers may be purchased in small units and tried, whereas, purchase of farm machinery, requires large investment and can't be tried in parts. The minikit demonstrations have helped in spreading the cultivation of high yielding variety crops as this method involves small scale trial by the farmers. Earlier adopters appear to be more concerned about the trialability of an innovation than later adopters.

Observability: the degree to which the results of an innovation and visible. The visible impact of an innovation facilitates its diffusion in the social system. For example, application of balanced fertilizer in crop plants has almost always been recommended to the farmers. In practice, farmers generally use more of nitrogenous fertilizers. It is because, the effect of nitrogenous fertilizers is very obvious in the eyes of the farmers – the plants 'jump', the leaves turn green, whereas, the effects of phosphatic and potassic fertilizers are not so evident. Understanding the beneficial effects of balanced fertilization by the farmers, which is more profitable in the long run, requires high level comprehension, which may be brought about by intensive training and communication.

Disease control has two aspects – preventive and curative. Preventive innovations in disease control are generally less costly than the curative innovations, but the results of preventive innovations are not so obvious, compared to those of the curative innovations. That is why technologies like treatment of seeds; preventive vaccinations etc. have been less adopted. Treatment of seed potato has, however, very high rate of diffusion, because preventing disease in this high investment crop brings higher return, i.e. has high relative advantage. The problem of lack of observability may; however be overcome by strengthening extension efforts like training, communication etc. which can enlarge one's vision and reasoning.

Predictability has also been perceived as an attribute of innovations (Napier, 1991). Predictability refers to the degree of certainty of receiving expected benefits from the adoption of an innovation. Substance farmers are often very cautious when making adoption decisions, because crop failure or substantial reduction in output due to failure of agricultural innovations to achieve expected production goals, can result in loss of meager landholdings and starvation of the family. Under such conditions farmers are reluctant to adopt any technology or technique which introduces a higher level of uncertainty into the operation of the farm enterprise.

It may be generalized that the attributes relative advantage, compatibility, trialability, observability and predictability of an innovation, as perceived by the members of a social system, are positively related to its rate of adoption. The complexity of an innovation, as perceived by the members of a social system, is negatively related to its rate of adoption.

By following Dube (1971), a few questions may be asked in respect of an innovation to determine its possibility of being adopted in a social system.

1. Does the innovation meet a felt need?
2. Do the people perceive any advantage in the innovation?
3. Is the innovation compatible with the situation and norms of the culture in which it is sought to be diffused?
4. Do people have the resources and facilities to adopt the innovation?
5. Can the people easily master the techniques involved in the innovation?
6. Does the gain from the adoption of the innovation- in terms of economic advantage, efficiency, prestige and so forth – adequately compensate the additional expenditure of money, time, labour etc. that its adoption may involve?

It replies to the questions are in the affirmative, the innovations is likely to be adopted soon.

Adoption: It is a decision to make full use of an innovation as a best course of action available.

Adoption Process: According to Rogers, "adoption process is the mental process through which an individual passes from hearing about an innovation to final adoption". Adoption process occurs at individual level.

The Adoption Process

> *"Ryan and Gross (1943), were probably the first to recognize that the adoption of a new idea consisted of stages. They distinguished between 'awareness' of hybrid seed corn, 'conviction' of its usefulness, trial 'acceptance' and 'complete adoption' of the innovation."*

Adoption is essentially a decision- making process. According to Johnson and Haver (1955), decision- making involves the following steps –

1. Observing the problem,
2. Making analysis of it,
3. Deciding the available courses of action,
4. Taking one course, and
5. Accepting the consequences of the decision.

Decision- making is a process which may be divided into a sequence of stages with a distinct type of activity occurring during each stage.

"The North Central Rural Sociology Subcommittee for the study of Diffusion of Form Practices (1955) identified five stages of the adoption process, which received world- wide attention."

These are –

1. Awareness,
2. Interest,
3. Evaluation,
4. Trial
5. Adoption.

According to them adoption is not an instantaneous act. It is a process that occurs over a period of time and consists of a series of actions.

Awareness Stage

The individual learns of the existence of the new idea but lacks information about it. At this stage an individual is aware of the idea, but lacks detailed information about it. For instance, the person may know only the name and may not know what the idea is, what it will do or how it will work.

Interest Stage

The individual develops interest in the innovation and seeks additional information about it. At this stage the individual develops interest in the idea and tries to acquire more information about it. The person wants to know what it is, how it works and what its potentialities are.

Evaluation Stage

The individual makes mental application of the new idea to the present and anticipated future situations and decides whether or not to try it. At this stage the individual judges the worth of innovation. The person makes an assessment whether the idea is applicable to own situation, and if applied what would be the result.

Trial Stage

The individual actually applies the new idea on a small scale in order to determine its utility in own situation. If, in the judgment of the individual the innovation has some plus points i.e. applicable to own situation, and if applied shall in some way or other be of advantage, the person takes a decision to try it. These are generally small scale trials to test the effectiveness of the innovation in one's own situation-apparently individuals need to test a new idea even though they have thought about it for long time and gathered information concerning it.

Adoption Stage

The individual uses the new idea continuously on a full scale. Trial may be considered as the practical evaluation of an innovation. It provides evidence of the advantages of the innovation. Being satisfied with the trial and considering the pros and cons of the situation, the individual takes a final decision and applies the innovation in a scale appropriate to own situation on a continued basis.

According to Singh (1965), the stages of adoption are dynamic and not static. The same five stages do not occur with all the adopters and all the practices. The sequence is not always the same. Sometimes one stage appears more than once. In some cases some stages are so short as to be imperceptible, and in other cases some stages seem to be skipped. There are no clear cut differences and sometimes the whole process is capsule and looks like a unit act. According to him the stages are –

Need: In this stage individual wishes the situation could be changed, expresses dissatisfaction and develops a compromise.

Awareness: The individual comes to know of something which is related to one's own need or arouse the interest. The person becomes acquainted with broad features of the innovation and knows the source of availability.

Interest: In this stage the individual tries to know more about the innovation. Asks extension agents or friends and seeks information and sees the innovation.

Deliberation: The individual mentally examines the possibility of application o f the innovation under own condition. Seeks advice of opinion leaders, observes the performance at different places and discusses with the members of the family. The individual then takes a decision to try not or reject the idea.

Trial: The individual puts the practice on a limited scale to observe the performance under own conditions.

Evaluation: The individual observes performance of the innovation on other's situation. Compares performance of the new with the old one and figures out other various dimensions collects data on the performance of the innovation on changes which will be necessary if the innovation is adopted. Calculates input- output, risks, uncertainties etc.

Adoption: In this stage the individual extends use of the innovation in the time and extent.

The innovation- Decision Process

According to Rogers (1983), the Innovation- Decision Process is the process through which an individual or other decision –making unit passes from first knowledge of an innovation, to forming an attitude towards the innovation, to a decision to adopt or reject, to implementation of the new idea, and to confirmation of this decision. This process consists of a series of actions and choices over time through which an individual or an organization evaluates a new idea and decides whether or not to incorporate the new idea into the ongoing practice. This behaviour consists essentially of dealing with the uncertainty that is inherently involved in deciding about a new alternative to those previously in existence. It is the perceived newness that is a distinctive aspect of innovation – decision making (compared to other types of decision making). Innovation – decision is a process that occurs over time and is conceptualized to have five stages.

Knowledge: occurs when an individual or other decision making unit is exposed to the innovation's existence and gains some understanding of how it functions. Knowledge function is mainly cognitive or knowing. Knowledge seeking is initiated by an individual and is greatly influenced by one's predispositions. Exposure is selective and, generally, an individual tends to expose to those ideas which are consistent with one's existing attitudes and belief, and avoids those which are in conflict with them. A need can motive an individual to seek information about an innovation and the knowledge of an innovation may develop the need.

In addition to the knowledge that an innovation exists, there may be two additional types of knowledge, how –to – do knowledge and principle – knowledge, That is, in addition to knowing that a particular new technology exists, a farmer would like to know how and why to use it.

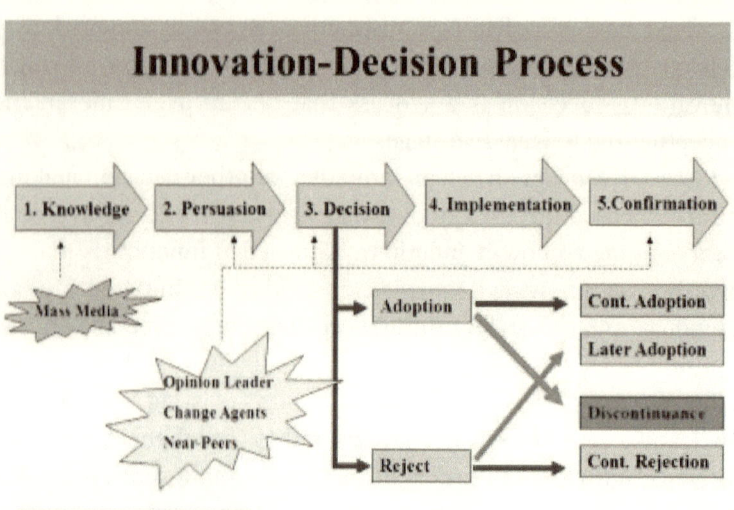

Innovation – Decision ProcessEnter Caption

Persuasion occurs when an individual or other decision making unit forms a favorable or unfavorable attitude towards the innovation. Persuasion function is mainly affective or related to feeling. At this stage the individual becomes more psychologically involved with the innovation and actively seeks information about it. The individual perceives the attributes of innovation, which is conditioned by one's personality and social system norms, and develops a general idea about the innovation.

In developing a favorable or unfavorable attitude towards the innovation, the individual may mentally apply the new idea to the present or anticipated future situations before deciding whether or not to try it. There may be two levels of attitudes, a specific attitude towards the innovation, and a general attitude towards change. A previous positive experience helps the process and a previous negative experience i.e. a failure develops resistance to future new ideas.

Decision occurs when an individual or other decision making unit engages in activities which lead to a choice to adopt or reject the innovation. The individual puts the innovation to a small- scale trial in own situation. Considering the relative advantage, risks involved and many other related factors like availability of market, need for the family etc. the individual takes a decision to adopt or reject the innovation.

Implementation occurs when an individual or other decision making unit puts an innovation into use. At this stage the individual is generally concerned with where to get the innovation, how to use it and what operational problems will be faced and how these could be solved. Implementation may involve changes in management of the enterprise and/ or modification in the innovation, to suit more closely to the specific needs of the particular person who adopts it.

Conformation occurs when an individual or other decision making unit seeks reinforcement of an innovation- decision already made, but may reverse this previous decision if exposed messages about the innovation. The decision to adopt or reject an innovation is not a terminal act. Human mind is in a dynamic state and an individual constantly evaluates the situation. If the individual perceives that the innovation is consistently giving satisfactory or unsatisfactory results, the person may continue to adopt or reject the innovation as the case may be, Reversal of the decision after adoption or rejection of an innovation may, however, take place at a later stage.

hroughout the confirmation stage, the individual seeks to avoid a state of internal disequilibrium or **Dissonance**, an uncomfortable state of mind, by reducing or eliminating it. An individual seeks to accomplish it by changing one's knowledge, attitude or actions.

Rejection is a decision not to adopt an innovation. Rejection may take two forms. Active rejection, which consists of considering adoption of the innovation (including even its trial), but then deciding not to adopt it. Passive rejection (also called non-adoption), which consists of never really considering use of the innovation.

Discontinuance is a decision to reject an innovation after having previously adopted it. Discontinuance may also take two forms. Replacement discontinuance is a decision to reject an idea in order to adopt a better idea that supersedes it. Disenchantment discontinuance is a decision to reject an idea as a result of dissatisfaction with its performance. Crop varieties generally deteriorate after a number of years. They are then replaced by superior varieties, if available, or may not be cultivated at all.

Over adoption

Sometimes it may happen that people continue to adopt an innovation, rather vigorously, when experts feel that it should not be so done. This is over adoption. An example of this phenomenon is indiscriminate sinking of shallow tube wells in a limited area, which may result in lowering of the water table, ultimately making the irrigation system ineffective. Excessive use of pesticides is another example of over adoption.

Over adoption produces negative effect, and may cause distortion or deterioration of the related systems. Insufficient knowledge about an innovation and inability to predict its consequences generally leads to over adoption. The role of extension agent is to prevent excessive adoption of the innovation, by providing adequate knowledge about the innovation and making the client system aware of its consequences. This may be achieved by appropriate surveillance, training and communication.

The Diffusion Effect

Not only does change agent effort have a different effect at different points in the sequence of an innovation's rate of adoption, but the system's self- generated pressure towards adoption also change as an increasing proportion of the members of the system adopt. This increasing pressure from interpersonal networks may be termed as the diffusion effect.

Consequences of innovation

Consequences are the changes that occur to an individual or to a social system as a result of the adoption or rejection of an innovation. There are at least three categories of consequences.

1. ***Desirable Vs. Undesirable Consequences:*** It depending on whether the effects of an innovation in a social system are functional or dysfunctional.
2. ***Direct Vs. Indirect Consequences:*** It depending on whether the changes to an individual or to a social system occur in immediate response to an innovation or as a second order result of the direct consequences of an innovation.
3. ***Anticipated Vs. Unanticipated Consequences:*** It depending on whether the changes are recognized and intended by the members of a social system or not.

Adopter Categories

All individuals in a social system do not adopt an innovation at the same time. Rather, they adopt in an ordered time sequence, and they may be classified into adopter categories on the basis of when they first begin using a new idea. In technology transfer programme, it is of great practical utility for the extension agents to identify the individuals who are likely to adopt innovations early and who may lag behind.

The adoption of an innovation over time follows a normal, bell-shaped curve when plotted over time on a frequency basis. If the cumulative number of adopters is plotted, it results in an S-shaped curve. The S-shaped curve rises slowly at first when there are few adopters in a time period, accelerates to a maximum when about half of the individuals in the system have adopted, and then increase at a gradually slower rate as the few remaining individuals finally adopt. The S-shaped curve is like that of a 'learning curve' as propounded by the psychologists. Each adoption in the social system is in a sense equivalent to learning trial by an individual.

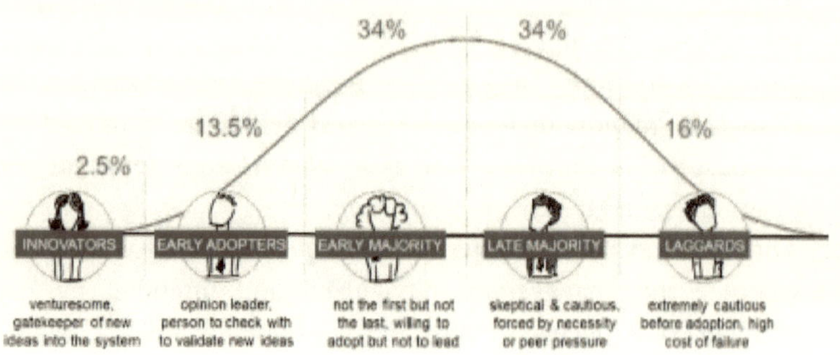

Adopter Categories

The distribution of adopters over time closely approaches normality, and may be explained by the statistical concept of normal curve. The distribution of the adopters may be partitioned into five adopter categories by using the mean and standard deviation. The area lying to the left of the mean time of adoption minus two standard deviations includes 2.5 percent of the individuals who are the first to adopt an innovation and are known as innovators. The next 13.5 percent between the mean minus one standard deviation and the mean minus two standard deviations to adopt the new idea are called as early adopters. The next 34 percent of the adopters between the mean time of adoption and mean minus one standard deviation are known as early majority. Between the mean and mean plus one standard deviation to the right of the mean are located the next 34 percent to adopt the new idea, the late majority. The last 16 percent to the right of mean plus one standard deviation are the last to adopt the innovation, the laggards. The five adopter categories are conceptualized as ideal types. The important characteristics of the adopter categories are mentioned in brief.

Innovators: They are venturesome and first to adopt a new idea, much ahead of other members in the community. They are generally very few in number. They must deviate from the social norm and may be viewed as deviants by others.

They are cosmopolite and their sphere of influence and activity may go beyond the community boundaries. They are mentally alert, have good contact with cosmopolite sources of information and actively seek new ideas. They are oriented to take risk, have large size enterprise and have the financial resource to absorb any possible loss due to adoption of the innovation. They are generally literate and have more prestige in the community.

The innovators are oriented to develop good contact with the research station and high level extension functionaries.

Early Adaptors: They are localite and are a more integrated part of the community. Because early adopters are not too far ahead, the average members of the community can comprehend their activities relating to adoption of the innovation. They have more opinion leadership and potential adopters look to them for advice and information about the innovation. They try to maintain adoption leadership to keep up their prestige in the community.

Early adopters are literate, have large size enterprise, high income, more participative and maintain good contact with cosmopolite sources of information. They do not test untried ideas, but quickest to use tried ideas in their own situations.

Early Majority: They adopt new ideas just before the average members of the community. They are neither very early nor relatively late to adopt an innovation. They are deliberate and take longer time to make the decision to adopt, in comparison to the innovators and early adopters. They do not hold leadership position in adoption, but actively participate in extension programmes like training, demonstration, farmer's day, study tour etc. They are slightly above average in education, social and economic status, and experience about the enterprise. Because of their limited resources, they cannot take hasty or poor decisions.

They have less contact with the cosmopolite sources of innovation. They are active localities and associate mainly with the people of their own community. They are the 'neighbours and friends' from whom majority of the members of the community seek information about innovations.

Late Majority: They are cautious and skeptical and adopt new ideas just after the average members of the community. They adopt mainly because people have, already adopted the innovation and getting the benefit out of it.

They have low level of education, low level of participation and depend mostly on localite sources of information.

Laggards: They are traditional and the last to adopt an innovation. By the time the laggards finally adopt an innovation, it may already have been superseded by a more recent idea which the innovators are already using.

They are most localite and primarily interact with those who have traditional values they tend to be frankly suspicious of innovators, and extension agents. A fast moving world is shocking to them and they find it difficult to adjust with it. They do not have opinion leadership and is almost a forgotten mass of people in the community. They have little or no education, least participant and hard if any contact with the outside world.

These people are likely to belong to the backward classes, may be working as sharecroppers and agricultural labourers, with very little land of their own. They are generally resource- poor people with little surplus to invest their production enterprise. They generally live in areas having least urban influence and, socially and economically the most disadvantaged.

Adoption behaviour is many times interpreted in terms of ability of the farmers to adopt a new technology. This interpretation may not be wholly correct as it does not take into account the lapses of research and extension. Technologies, for the development and dissemination of which there have been very little dialogue with the farmers, are less likely to be adopted, particularly by the resource-poor farmers. The dialogue between the proponents and participants provides an opportunity for exchange of information and experience to reach mutual understanding and is considered essential for adoption of a technology by the client system.

Factors Influencing Rate of Adoption of Innovations

It is apparent that adoption is the decision to adopt or reject an innovation. The adoption behaviour of an individual farmer is influenced by various factors. Following are some important factors.

- *Social Factors*
- *Personal Factors*
- *Situational Factors*

Social Factors

Community standards and social relationships provide the general framework wherein the process of change occurs and they account for the differences between one communities with that of other.

Social Values: Social values differ from group to group and community to community. The extent to which changes are adopted depends on the values and expectations of the group and upon the extent to which the individual is expected to confirm.

Local leadership: The acceptance of change is also influenced by the nature of leadership and control in the group or community. In some communities, none would accept a new idea, unless the leader in the community accepts the idea. If he accepts, he will influence all other farmers in the community to accept.

Social contact: The nature and extent of social contact within and outside the community is important in the diffusion of new ideas and techniques as indicated below.

1. **Nature of social contact:** The presence of organizations whose objectives include the promotion of changes will aid directly in the diffusion process. On the other hand, where social contacts are primarily through kinship, visiting and informal activities, there may be greater resistance to change.
2. **Extent of Social contact:** The extent to which social contacts are confined to the immediate locality is a factor. Higher the social

orientation of the people, the more likely they are to accept new ideas.

Social Distance: The social distance associated with wide status differences are also a factor in the diffusion of farm information through inter- personal channels. For example, tenant farmer in some areas may not get ideas from the large farm owners because of their lack of contact. Also small farmers may fail to communicate with big farmers.

Personal Factors: Some people adopt new ideas and practices more quickly than others because of differences in the characteristics of individuals as detailed below.

1. **Age:** In general, elderly farmers seem to be somewhat less inclined to adopt new practices than younger ones.
2. **Education:** Many research studies conducted in social science revealed that higher the level of education more will be the rate of adoption of innovation.
3. **Psychological characteristics:** Exposure to reliable sources of farm information may create a state of rationality which in-turn predisposes an individual to the adoption of new practices. A mentally flexible person has higher adoption rates than one with mental rigidity. Some people are found to be more prone to change than others.
4. **Values and attitudes (Cultural Characteristics):** Values found to be positively related to farm practices adoption are; a desire by farmers and their wives for a high school or college education for their children a high emphasis on science and material comfort and also wide contacts within and beyond the community. A high emphasis on traditionalism, isolationism and security has been found to be negatively associated with adoption of improved practices.

Situational Factors: Some farmers adopt farm practices more quickly at one time than others relate to the situation in which they find themselves.

1. **The nature of the practices:** The speed with which adoption will take place is partly dependent on the nature of practices itself.
2. **Complexity:** In general the more complex a practice, the more slowly it will be adopted. The following classification of practices in terms of their complexity roughly represents the decreasing order of speed with which acceptance may be expected to occur.
3. **A simple change:** A change in materials and equipments only without a change in technique or operations.
4. **Improved practices:** Change in existing operations with or without a change in materials or equipment e.g. change in cropping pattern.
5. **Innovation:** Change involving new techniques or operations e.g. drip irrigation. vi. Change in total enterprise: e.g. from crop to livestock farming.
6. **Cost:** Those practices with little cost seem to be adopted more rapidly than those which are more expensive. E.g. Organic fertilizers locally available.
7. **Net returns:** Those practices which yield the greatest managerial returns per rupee invested and in the shortest time seem to be adopted most rapidly.
8. **Relative advantage:** Comparative advantage. E.g. Tractors efficacy higher than bullock power.
9. **Compatibility:** E.g. The lack of compatibility of beef rearing for meat with cultural values in many parts of India.
10. **Trialability (Divisibility):** New ideas that can be tried on a small scale basis will generally be adopted more rapidly than innovations that are not divisible. (E.g) New seeds or fertilizers can be tried on a small scale but new machinery cannot be tried.
11. **Observability (Communicability):** It is the degree to which the results of an innovation may be diffused to others. The results of some practices are easily observed while the results of some

innovations are not easily observed. E.g. Application of nitrogenous fertilizers to plants.

12. **Farm Income:** High farm income associated with high adoption levels.

13. **Size of farm:** Size of farm is always positively related to the adoption of new farm practices.

14. **Tenurial Status:** The adoption of innovations is more among the owner cultivators than tenant cultivators.

15. **Sources of farm information used:** Higher the degree of contact with information sources, higher will be the rate of adoption of innovations. A high positive correlation is particularly evident with the use of sources as government agencies. High dependence on relatives and friends as sources of information is usually negatively associated with the adoption of new farm practices.

16. **Levels of Living:** Since successful farm practice adoption is instrumental in providing the means of supporting a higher level of living, a positive correlation between the two would be expected and is generally found.

References:

1. Adebo Simon (2000).Training Manual on Participatory Rural Appraisal.

2. Dipak De, Basavaprabhu Jirli,2010. A Handbook of Extension Education. Agrobios (INDIA), Jodhpur. P- 31-48.

3. Grover Indhu 2004. Technical writing, in Handbook of Communication and Media, (eds.) Indhu Grover, Nishi Sethi and Deepak Grover. Agrotech Publishing Academy, Udaipur.

4. http://ecoursesonline.iasri.res.in/

5. http://www.fao.org/participation/tools/PRA.html

6. http://www.smallstock.info/issues/participation.html

7. Kumar Krishna.(1996).Rapid Rural Appraisal Methods. The World Bank, Washington.

8. Meenambigai, J. 2011. Reading manual on Communication and Information Technology. Department of Agricultural Extension, Faculty of Agriculture, Annamalai University, Annamalai Nagar

131